P9-BJO-727

COMMUNITY, JUNIOR, AND TECHNICAL COLLEGES

A PUBLIC RELATIONS SOURCEBOOK

COMMUNITY, JUNIOR, AND TECHNICAL COLLEGES

A PUBLIC RELATIONS SOURCEBOOK

William A. Harper

Vice President for Communications
American Association of Community and Junior Colleges
Washington, D.C.

WITHDRAWN

HEMISPHERE PUBLISHING CORPORATION

Washington   London

Hemisphere Publishing Corporation
1025 Vermont Ave., N.W., Washington, D.C.   20005

1 2 3 4 5 6 7 8 9 0   TS TS   7 8 3 2 1 0 9 8 7

Library of Congress Cataloging in Publication Data

Harper, William A
Community, junior, and technical colleges.

Includes index.
1. Community colleges—United States.   2. Junior
colleges—United States.   3. Trade schools—United
States.   4. Public relations—Universities and colleges
—United States.   I. Title.
LB2328.H36   659.2'9'37873   77-1993
ISBN 0-89116-043-4

Printed in the United States of America

Contents _____

3 INTEGRATING THE PARTS   45

4 ORGANIZATION AND STAFF   71

5 A FAMILY PROCESS   97

9 IN CONCLUSION—A CHALLENGE TO THE PRESIDENT   197

Foreword ─────────────────────

It is fortunate that this book has come along at this time. There is a dearth of literature about the community/ junior college generally, and within that field very little guidance has been provided in public relations. Yet, while I cannot cite quantitative research for support, it is my belief that failure in the execution of basic public relations skills has been a leading cause of crises in American colleges and the attendant recycling of administrators.

We tend to think of higher education generally and the community/junior college specifically as a noble calling, a mission in which highly trained professionals provide quality educational services to our citizens. It is both of those. Therefore, we train our professionals in techniques of identifying educational needs and in devising instructional strategies to meet those needs. We believe that, if we have done a good job of teaching and counseling, we have done our job.

The fact is that this is not the case. The American community/junior college does not operate in splendid isolation. Instead, it is situated in an American community. That community has private interest groups making conflicting demands on the college. It has layers of government which compete with the college for public dollars and seek to control its growth and destiny. It has voters who, in most cases, provide or withhold the money which is the very lifeblood of the institution. It has students who, although they may be well educated, may also be both unhappy and talkative. So, while public relations receives little attention in our graduate schools of education and is not blessed with a massive body of literature, it is of crucial importance to faculty members, administrators, board members—to everyone who has a stake in the health of higher education.

William Harper's experience as the public relations expert in the Washington office of the American Association of Community and Junior Colleges makes him admirably qualified to author this book. He is engaged in the day-to-day practice of public relations; at the same time, he is intimately familiar with the nature of the American community/junior college. Here, he has drawn together both the basic theory of public relations and the practical application of that theory to the operation of this unique institution. These pages are rich in the communication of his years of experience.

In a brief twenty years, the community/junior college has risen from its apprenticeship in the educational community to its present position as the leading deliverer of postsecondary education in the United States. With this new status comes great responsibility to work with governments, with private groups, and with the general public in a skillful and mature manner. With this volume, William Harper has made that job easier. I commend him and his book to you.

Bill J. Priest
Chancellor, Dallas County
Community College District
Dallas, Texas

Preface _____

This book is offered in the interest of advancing the cause of postsecondary education—particularly as represented by community and junior colleges, technical institutes, vocational education centers, and independent schools. It is based on the premise that effective public relations insures understanding and appreciation that will result in full use of resources by postsecondary institutions and at once generate needed financial and moral support. The need for well-organized communications systems has become more pronounced as society on the one hand and the educational institutions on the other have grown more complex. At the same time, the competition for attention, as well as support, among deserving agencies and organizations is, like it or not, a fact of life. It is a fact that community-based educational centers must face up to as they attempt to expand services and contributions to the cities and towns and rural areas that they serve.

There is a paucity of information directed specifically at planners, administrators, and policy makers with regard to public relations problems and how to organize programs to deal with them. I have tried here to bridge some of the informational gaps and to stimulate greater attention to this important area of administration. These writings are designed to answer some questions—and to raise others that can best be resolved by discussion and planning at the institutional level. They are presented in a spirit of service to post-secondary education.

I am grateful to the American Association of Community and Junior Colleges for a special leave policy that provided time and opportunity to pursue this work. Appreciation is also expressed to the Fenwick Island Surfing Team: Scott Rickards, Timothy Harper, Jack Powell, Ken Roughton, Mark Harper, Ross Cropper, Les Corby and honorary members Margaret Harper and Kathryn Harper.

William A. Harper

Changing Environment _____1

"What was your first year at the community college like," I asked the young man.

"Well, I enjoyed it pretty much," he replied. "I guess it was like the thirteenth year of high school. But the courses were a little tougher and I had more freedom."

He thought for a moment, then added, "Some of my friends who went to universities have put me down for staying in town and going to the local college. I guess they think I'm some kind of dummy who couldn't get in anywhere else.

"And that's just not true. My dad is building a new house, money was short, and I thought I could help out by going to the local college. It's a lot cheaper and I have been able to help out at home."

What this bit of dialog suggests is that the community college remains one of the most misunderstood arms of postsecondary education in America. Many of the clients aren't really sure whether they ought to be there—and their misgivings are fed by the deprecatory views of others who aren't there. No doubt those who complete their programs, go on to decent jobs, or transfer to other institutions will later look back on the experience with appreciation. Many will become supporters instead of doubters at a time when their support will do the most good for the institution.

Meanwhile, however, the community college may find it more difficult to obtain and retain accreditation; it may find it harder to get the best teachers. State legislatures will

3

constantly have to be reconvinced of the value of the institution. Battles for federal aid will continue to be fought repeatedly in the halls of Congress. Then the federal agencies will have to be persuaded to release necessary funds, to give community college proposals due consideration.

This is not to suggest that community colleges are beleaguered—up against a wall of indifference and unconcern. As many newspaper headlines have put it, community colleges have grown up; they have nearly lost the appellation of junior. They are now part and parcel of the American educational scene; there is no mistaking that fact. Having arrived at that point of acceptance, however, they face even stiffer competition for support in the face of new constraints on spending for education and of public disenchantment with ever-increasing demands on their tax dollars. The bad times, the recession of the early 1970s, economic crises in the states and cities, will have a lasting affect on community college efforts to realize their full promise and potential in American society.

TO BE GOOD IS TO BE RIGHT

While there are many who entertain doubts about the community college, the general view is that this kind of institution is good for the country. It was especially good in the sixties and seventies when America suffered some of its most devastating social conflicts. When cities were in upheaval as blacks demanded greater equality in all things. When Chicanos and native Americans cried out for educational programs appropriate to their needs. When women sought a new place in the power structures of the country. When vast numbers of Americans railed at the high cost of war in money and lives.

Perhaps it was mere coincidence; perhaps it was by grand design. Whatever the reason, the community college blossomed in the sixties. It was an open-door institution. Since education traditionally has been tied to employment and professional success, the opening of college doors to all was a giant step forward in the battle for equality. Whether merely a fortuitous happenstance or a well-planned maneuver, the community college came into its own at a time when nothing could have been more advantageous to a country seething with turmoil and trouble. It was good for the country.

There are those who would assume that being good is being right. And if a thing is good, and it's therefore right, then it will be supported; it will be heralded; it will engender, merely by being good and right, the kind of relations that will result in approbation. But one must take into account the fact that the community college came into its own at a time when people were questioning any and all institutions, when the total system was being viewed with vigorous skepticism. Just because it was fresh and "good" was not enough. There were those who questioned how good it was, and therefore how right it was.

At the height of the San Francisco State College riots, a black leader came on CBS television demanding to know, "What kind of equal educational opportunity are we getting? We are being relegated to the second-rate institution known as the junior college. That's the kind of equalization we are getting." Even educational pundits were referring to community colleges as dumping grounds, second-rate colleges, purveyors of inferior education, high schools with ashtrays. The community college was a put-on. It was high school extended. It was tinkertoy university. It was certainly not college. And to many, it was not good and not right.

In short, a major mistake was made in planning and

conceptualizing the community college. The error was to be found in the assumption that, by just being there, by saying, "Here's your community college; come and get it," there would be approval, receptiveness, instant response, thorough understanding. People did come in great numbers. This new institution represented new hope for many. But what attitudes did they come with—and what attitudes were they to take away?

There is no question but that the community colleges in those booming sixties were successful, certainly in terms of numbers: Numbers of people. Numbers of dollars spent. Numbers of new buildings erected. Numbers of new programs created. It was a numbers game of the highest order for the writers, speechmakers, and critics dealing with the phenomenon known as the community college. But the numbers game eventually plays itself out. Numbers do not make a satisfactory base for progress and advancement. During the boom, the big question was how can we build enough classrooms, get enough teachers (hundreds of thousands were called for), and create necessary parking spaces to take care of the avalanche of persons that need and want to be accommodated. Ten years later, the planners are looking at vacant spaces, wondering where the new students will come from, cutting back on faculty—coping with a whole new set of numbers problems. So numbers do not beget success.

Analogous to the community college story may be that of educational television. Television was discovered as a natural medium for teaching in the 1950s. Here was a medium that captured the imagination, that was available to almost every home, that was made to order for education. Multimillions could be reached by a flick of the switch. National committees were formed to promote educational television. Foundations poured millions of dollars into programming. Communities raised funds to build and back installation of the electronic equipment and studios needed to carry out the newly found educational mission. Great teachers came forward to spread wisdom by the tube. Hundreds of educational channels were envisioned.

Today, there are fewer than three hundred educational television stations on the air. Many are on the air only sporadically, and much of the programming is classified as public service rather than instructional or formally educational. There have been some notable successes in individual educational programs, and many Americans have actually received college degrees or high school diplomas via television.

Educational television is not a flop, but it has never quite realized its promise. The multimillions will not give up the all-American family show, the shoot-em-up westerns, or the midnight talk programs for education. A new day may come with cable TV or satellite broadcasting, but it is still a long way off. The point is, the numbers game did not work. Television did not become the panacea for all the educational ills of the country. It made some impact and will, it is hoped, continue to provide another dimension for the educational system of the country.

NEED FOR A PROGRAM

No question about it, the community college is generally considered to be a "good" thing. There are critics and questioners, but there is mounting evidence that this kind of institution was needed and helped to answer cries for universal opportunity for education beyond high school. It has grown to be a significant factor in the educational fabric of the country. The concept is even spreading to

other countries, perhaps in formats different from those of
the United States.

But to be fully effective, the institution must be well
understood. Voters will not continue indefinitely to provide
financial assistance unless they understand and appreciate
what the money is doing for them as a community. The
private sector will not come forward with aid unless there
is understanding. The congress will not continue to intro-
duce bills and debate their value if it does not know that
what is being supported is right.

So it is not good enough just to be there. Word-of-
mouth, occasional speeches by the chief administrator, a
chance editorial will not provide the kind of information
and background necessary to bring about the understanding
and appreciation that will generate the necessary support.
Major industry learned long ago that, in a complex society,
it is not enough just to have a good product; that good
product must beg for attention among other, similar products that may not be as good, though better known.

Remember the Edsel. One bad product, its time not yet
come, cost Ford Motor Company credibility and support
for all of its other products. It could not rely on its
reputation as a builder of good products in general. Something had to be done to offset the bad publicity of that
one major aberration. What it took to do that was a
massive public relations and advertising program that soon
put the Edsel behind Ford and brought public attention
back into focus on what Ford really was: a corporation of
integrity; producer of good, if not fine, products; a company with tradition, history, and American technological
and management know-how behind it; a company that could
take the fun that was poked at it, absorb the great financial
losses accruing to that one mistake, and go on to make
bigger (or smaller) and better cars.

Fortunately, the community college has not yet suffered a major aberration; as an institution, it has not yet made a big mistake. The concept, like all the things that are considered good in America, is one against which it is difficult to muster an argument. If education can be made more widely available, then surely Americans will be better for it. But the community college does exist in a competitive situation. It is anathema to many to talk about competition in education. Each institution has its place, they say, and there is no need for competitive attitudes and actions. Anathema or not, the notion will not wash.

Any community college that opens in a major city will draw off many students from the local private college or university. It will get some of the money, both from public and private sources, that might have gone to the other institutions. As civic leaders take an interest in it, other institutions will compete for their support. In short, the community college does operate in an increasingly competitive society where the recipe for support must be cut into increasingly smaller portions as various good things in the society vie for attention and assistance. What can happen is acutely dramatized by the curtailment, in New York, of free education beyond high school, as the city struggled for survival.

While the community college has not produced an Edsel, has not made a universal mistake that calls the whole concept into question, it does have constant public relations or community relations problems that require finesse and sophisticated handling. Regrettably, these institutions have not had the expertise and organized programs of public relations that would have saved them headaches, stalled advancement of their programs, and resistance to innovation and experimentation. Lack of appropriate public relations programs have unquestionably held community colleges back.

Let's cite a hypothetical example of what lack of sophistication in the public relations could do to retard progress for a college. The institution, located in a medium-sized town, has decided to launch a very forward-looking program in prison education. It will do two things: (1) take programs to the local prison for the inmates and (2) bring some model prisoners to the home campus. At a time of growing concern for what was happening in correctional institutions, this bold program seemed a natural contribution. Unfortunately, there was no well planned advance campaign to inform the public of what was about to take place, to elicit public opinion, and to bring about understanding of the enterprise. In fact, the effort was begun in virtual secrecy. Nothing can be secret in a public enterprise. Word of the program leaked out. Citizens were aghast; young Christian youth would be going to class side by side with felons, with murderers, with outcasts of society. There was a great hue and cry. Newspapers, while generally in favor of the program, were forced to soft-pedal their stand because of the overwhelming outcry against the project. Before it was over, the president came near to resigning; there were student protests that disrupted classes for days (the students naturally favored the program); the board of trustees were divided; the whole process of education was in chaos. Eventually, wiser heads prevailed, the facts were aired, and the public was won over. But at what cost to the college and its community?

Not only was the campus in disruption for months, but any new program mentioned since was cause for suspicion. Some of the personal wounds resulting from the situation will never be healed. There are those who will never again trust the president and some other administrators. Local media tend to be more critical and raise more questions about how the college is spending public money.

This situation occurred in a college that had, at the time, an administrative assistant to the president trained in educational administration but not experienced in public relations. Yet his was the guiding public relations advice. He carried under his job description all responsibility for college relations. Had this institution taken the time and trouble—lots of time—to assume the care and feeding of appropriate information to the public prior to launching the prisoner education program, the reprehensible situation that arose could have been ameliorated if not avoided entirely.

In fact, it would not be inappropriate to suggest that, had there been an effective public relations program, the prison education activity could have been launched with great civic approval and support which would have provided far more assurance of success. On the other hand, the time may not yet have been ripe for what was then a truly advanced step in education. If all other activity is to be hampered by one somewhat questionable program, then perhaps the prudent thing to do is to postpone it until supporters are adequately prepared for the innovation in question.

The above situation has been made up and is deliberately exaggerated to sharply point up the dangers of poor public relations planning or lack of it. Any reader who questions the validity of it can substitute many reports, from back issues of *The Chronicle of Higher Education,* of true-life situations involving such matters as administrative-faculty conflict, unpopular educational programs, and questionable expenditures of public funds. Obviously, not all such problems can be blamed on ineffective public relations, but lack of proper communications almost always exacerbates what is already a bad condition.

Unfortunately, there are far too many such examples,

enough to justify the conclusion that community colleges, while often and perhaps most of the time cognizant of the needs of the people, do not have the enterprise, staff, and foresight to generate proper understanding and appreciation for the job to be done. It is something of a mystery to me that community colleges, theoretically in and of the community, have not given necessary attention to the tools and techniques of community or public relations. Perhaps the answer is, as I have said, that those responsible feel that it is enough to be good, that good makes right.

NEGLECT OF PUBLIC RELATIONS

Public relations in community colleges are now at a point where they were in state colleges and universities twenty to thirty years ago: Drum beaters were not to be tolerated; there was something suspicious about the function. A state college was a good thing. Why would it need to use Madison Avenue techniques, publicists, and flim flam to bring in students and support? It was unthinkable. Though public relations people were employed and operative in the four-year institutions, their positions were often disguised under some nondescript title. Witness the case of a college which employed a top publicist under the title of "general secretary." Her job was well understood by the local media, by students, by faculty and administrators. She even became president of the American College Public Relations Association, the national professional organization for practitioners (now the Council for the Advancement and Support of Education). But her work was hamstrung because it was not officially recognized for what it was, little money could be turned her way for budgeting purposes, and she had to spend a great deal of time covering up the good work she was doing.

That, of course, has changed in the state colleges and universities. It would be difficult to search out a four-year college or university without at least two persons working in public relations, operating under reasonably healthy budgets. Medium-sized colleges and universities employ from five to ten persons in all the aspects of college relations work. Some major universities have thirty to forty persons under hire, fluctuating, of course, as needs dictate. Community colleges, for reasons that are difficult to discern, remain public relations shy; frequently their public relations directors are English or journalism teachers carrying college relations duties as collateral activities.

In some colleges, the president's secretary serves as the college relations representative, fields questions from newspapers, talks to civic leaders, schedules speeches, and in general handles public relations matters. The presidential secretary is a key person in the college and knows about many things that go on in the institution, but can that person be expected to interpret policy, explain the workings of the presidential pulse, and speak out on the latest protest? It is an untenable situation for the secretary and for the college.

There are those who feel that the president is really the public relations functionary, for it is he or she who is most competent, most knowledgeable about the institution and its ways and means, who can speak out most effectively, and who can thus chart appropriate programs in public relations. After all, the president is the leader, paid to be the voice of the college, paid to take the lumps along with the kudos, paid to put the college's best foot forward, paid to get it all together so that there will be a good image.

No president is paid enough to do all that, and few presidents are equipped to handle public relations along with facilities planning, academic direction, faculty development and leadership, management of board relations, collective bargaining, curriculum development, and the myriad responsibilities that fall under his or her purview. True, the president does speak for the college, but he may need advice and counsel on when and what to say, and how to say it. Just as he must have support from well-trained and educated academicians to plan the transfer program, and assistance from expert vocational education personnel to work up the occupational program, so he should have proper assistance in carrying out the public relations program of the institution.

There are many so-called public relations responsibilities that a president can and probably must perform. It will be necessary to give some key speeches. He or she will find it important to communicate with local political leaders or state legislators. It may be appropriate, as judged by expert public relations staff, for the president to give testimony before legislative hearings or even congressional hearings, but what goes into these addresses and testimonials may well be outlined and even prepared by backup people on the president's staff. These are the more high-level, the more exciting public relations activities. Few presidents are prepared to or should be involved in the nitty-gritty day-to-day, month-to-month, year-to-year public relations. Presidents should not be involved, except in a peripheral way, in the preparation of press releases, publications, special events, and the other fundamental things that go on in a good public relations program.

Of course most presidents, no matter how omniscient they may feel, are not trained or educated for the routine work in public relations. Nor should they be expected to be, except in the sense of being knowledgeable about the part the routine public relations work plays in advancing and promoting the role of the institution in the community. If the president does not understand the value of the activity, then it follows that there will be no program of consequence. This is probably one of the reasons that community colleges are not well staffed and well organized in public relations.

"Don't rock the boat," seems to reflect the presidential attitude on many college campuses. I know of an instance in which a president discouraged public notice of an important though innocuous event on the campus. He seemed to operate on the theory that the press would dig in and find something, anything, questionable about any special event, activity, or program. His rule, therefore, was to avoid calling attention to anything.

This is not a put-down of presidents; it is only meant to indicate that their burdens are far too great for them to be encumbered with the additional task of carrying out a public relations program that is proved to be the baliwick of professionals. In fact, there are many administrators who have the savvy, the knack, for doing everything right, for taking a leading role in public relations at no expense to their other duties, but where this kind of administrator is found, is also found a healthy backup staff in public relations. It is also fair to note that, though chief administrators are often expected to carry out this function, and certainly to understand it, there is rarely anything in their training or background to help them win friends and influence people. Many of the newer, younger presidents have come out of university leadership training programs. These programs do not generally include course work in public relations.

It is no wonder then that community relations remains somewhat neglected in community colleges, with secretaries often fielding important policy questions, English teachers writing press releases in their spare time, and board members making public pronouncements when good public relations counsel would advise them to remain silent.

WRONG IMAGE BLURS NEED FOR PUBLIC RELATIONS

There is a persistent fallacy about community colleges—part of the image problem—that is often enunciated. It goes like this: Why should a little community college have a high powered public relations staff? The notion persists that community colleges are generally small and relatively insignificant. When all the bodies are counted, however, we are talking about institutions that range in size from one thousand to thirty thousand, with the average being from two thousand to five thousand. Small institutions? Hardly. Insignificant institutions? Hardly.

Community colleges are not small, and in most cases they are growing and expanding, even at a time when there is shrinkage in college-going generally. The institutions are complex, offering as they do a great variety of programs and attempting to integrate these into a workable whole. They are also serving an intricate mix of people—often a microcosm of society itself—accompanied by myriad problems in human and social relations. They are exciting, carving out new programs which have never existed before, experimenting with new learning devices and techniques, trying out new class schedules, and keeping facilities open in many cases around the clock. Their budgets are big and complicated. They must be accountable, perhaps more than any other kind of higher education institution, for how they spend the taxpayers' dollars, because those taxpayers are looking over the shoulders of the planners.

Significant? John Gardner noted that the community college is the most revolutionary concept to come along in the last half of the twentieth century. The impact that these institutions have made on the nation's manpower needs, its service to minorities, and its leadership in open education suggests a truly significant impact on American society. Being big, and growing, being complex, being significant, calls for a high degree of sophistication in college relations.

As earlier suggested, no institution feels a greater sense of the need for accountability than does the community college. Accountability is, in a sense, a public relations matter, not merely a matter for bookkeepers, accountants, and auditors. It calls for clarification, interpretation, and dissemination of information. It has to do with the people's right to know. So a public relations program that will shed light on the workings of the institution, its failures as well as it successes, is essential to ensuring accountability to the public which it serves. A good public relations program will not hide, cannot obscure, mistakes. It will call attention to the good as well as to the bad, but it will approach the job in a positive, aggressive way that will show that something can be gained, something can be learned, future problems can be avoided by public knowledge that the institution can make mistakes. It is a question of palatability as well as accountability.

COMMUNITY SERVICE VERSUS
PUBLIC RELATIONS

Let us go on to another fallacy that pertains in any consideration of the public relations activity in a community college. It has to do with the term, and the activity known as, community service. In recent years, community service has become a watchword of the community college. Books have been written about it. Conferences have been

held on it. Cults have sprung up around it. It has become, in a sense, the lifeblood of the community college. Old fashioned terms such as continuing education and extension service have been subordinated to the term community service. Under the rubric of community service come the many aspects of outreach, off-campus activities, recreational programs, cultural events, community counseling, and extension of the formal classroom into far corners of the community. Courses in correctional institutions, day-care centers, centers for the aging, mobile counseling units, job placement centers, education on military bases, and just about anything else that goes beyond the formal classroom situation fit under community service.

It is a dimension of which the community college can be most proud. In fact, from a public relations standpoint, it is among the most saleable, most visible, most exciting vehicle that the college has to offer. It sets this kind of institution off from most other kinds of postsecondary education units, which tend to be more formal and more traditional, more conventional and more conservative in carrying out their particular educational missions. Too often, however, community service is confused with community relations (i.e., public relations); it is considered to be synonymous with community relations. Often the director or dean of community service is also considered to be the director of public relations, and he is usually an educator, not a public relations professional.

The fact is that the community service operation should be maintained and considered on a level with that of any other large educational department of the college. Its job is to provide educational programs and services in unusual ways and unusual places, to take new approaches to what is essentially another learning and service arm of the institution. It should receive no more or no less attention from public relations than it deserves and should not take away from other areas of college service.

If community service, therefore, is taken to be synonymous with community relations, then the institution may suffer. Other departments, other services, and other activities may be neglected, if not overlooked, if the community services department doubles as the public relations department. This is inappropriate and to be avoided. It would not be overstating the case to suggest that not all community service is good community relations. A public relations professional, sitting apart from community service or any other department, may on occasion have to counsel against the establishment or initiation of certain kinds of community services. Whether this counsel is acted upon is not the question. The public relations man or woman must be in a position apart, from which he or she can be objective when offering advice to any department on the viability and acceptability of certain programs. No purpose is served when a learning program is simply not acceptable to the public. The community service director will certainly fight for his department and its program over all others; that, after all, is his bread and butter and the thing to which he is committed. Thus, he cannot be expected to function also as the objective evaluator of programs to be initiated and the service to be offered.

Beyond the matter of services that may or may not be acceptable, there is the question of day-to-day public relations. If the community services director has responsibility for public relations as well, it would only be human to neglect other aspects of the college program in the zeal to promote and develop the community services dimension. While community service work obviously lends itself more appropriately to public relations visibility than any other aspect of the educational activity, that is even more reason to recommend that public relations be a separate entity.

Guidelines for Chapter 1 ―――――――――

The main thrust of this chapter has been to set a backdrop for planning and outlining appropriate public relations programs for community-based postsecondary educational institutions. There is an obvious need for development of better programs and for constant, consistent attention to relations with various audiences and publics at local, state, and national levels. In referring frequently to the community college, it should be understood that what applies to that kind of two-year institution will have meaning as well for vocational-technical schools, technical institutes, two-year branches of universities, and private and proprietary institutions that emphasize service to community.

Here are some guidelines:

1. Community-based educational institutions are good for the society, but there must be an organized effort to inform, clarify, and interpret the role and functions of the institutions.
2. Community institutions exist in a competitive society. They must vie for attention that will beget support, both moral and financial.
3. Community-based postsecondary institutions of higher education are accepted, as witness their vigorous

growth and development in the past twenty years, yet there must be fuller understanding if progress is to be made in fulfilling promise and potential.

4. The institutions must increasingly be more accountable to those who support them. Public relations plays a significant role in the business of accountability.

5. The newer institutions of postsecondary education stand in public relations about where state colleges and universities stood twenty to thirty years ago. They must take immediate steps to organize and staff for the function.

6. Community-based institutions suffer from the fallacious notion that they are not big enough or complex enough to require a well-planned public relations effort. This notion must be dispelled in the interest of advancement.

7. Community-based institutions tend to place too great a share of the public relations function on the shoulders of already over-burdened chief administrators. Professionals should be employed to alleviate this situation.

8. Community service is too often confused with community relations. These activities are not synonymous. Community relations should be a separate function of management.

9. The community-based two-year institutions of postsecondary education can make greater impact and contribute more importantly to society if they are better understood. Goals of community relations should be synonymous with those of the institution.

Opportunities—
Not Problems _____2

"You asked me what is required in this job," said Fred. "It's simple. All that is necessary is to get the board of directors, singly or as a group, in the newspapers or on radio and television about once every two weeks."

"You're joking," I said, "This big suburban institution must have a helluva lot of public relations problems and opportunities beyond mere publicity for the board."

"Sure it does," Fred replied, "but the essential task so far as the administration and board are concerned is to get publicity for the board. I should say favorable publicity. Nothing else really counts. It's a political thing.

"And that," Fred went on, "is why I am getting out. There just isn't any real understanding of public relations, no support for it. And there's absolutely no professional challenge for me."

Not only is the myopic view of this college resulting in the loss of a top-notch public relations man with twenty years of experience and an excellent reputation, but it is also eroding public confidence in the institution. Oh yes, the college will survive. It may even grow and prosper. But it will do so amidst a welter of problems that might have been avoided with a public relations program that goes beyond promotions of the board of trustees.

This case is an extreme example of the treatment, or lack of it, of the public relations function in the community college. But far too often, the view of what public relations is all about is extremely narrow, even to the point of considering it a necessary evil. The public relations man or woman is, often as not, treated with suspicion: he or she is not to be trusted. The public relations professional, through his performance, achievement, and acumen, can help to alleviate this problem of trust. But the burden of support lies with chief administrators, trustees, even local civic leaders who play a role in college development and planning. These participants in the college enterprise must have a thorough understanding of the management role of public relations.

THE REAL JOB

Perhaps the difficulty is one of terminology. Public relations is usually thought of in terms of *problems*—of putting out fires, creating defenses against criticism, covering up activities that some publics may have questions about. No doubt about it—the public relations function does, on frequent occasions, call for problem solving with regard to public opinion, and that is not an ignoble task if properly executed. It is a matter of bringing all the facts to bear on a particular controversial problem in order to open and maintain channels of communication with important publics and bring about equilibrium in thinking and discussion of institutional problems.

It would be far more appropriate, though, to look upon public relations in terms of *opportunities*. Rather than sit back and wait for the problems to arise or mayhem to break loose, the public relations man should be constantly on the lookout for opportunities to present the best, the real, side of the college to the public. He or she will find that the opportunities are inexhaustible, that the chances to project an image of a forward-looking, contributory program are limitless. Looking for opportunities in just one aspect of public relations—public information—there are countless stories that exist on every campus:

- the middle-aged mother who enrolls in college after rearing a large family—and the community-based institution provided the opportunity
- the high school dropout who, after wandering aimlessly and forlornly for two years, turns to the community college, and the doors are open to him
- the faculty member who has found a new way to get the message across and made it more meaningful—because the institution allowed him to do it
- the creation of a new occupational education program that shows promise of bringing new industry to the community
- the elderly citizen who leaves the rocking chair to take up pottery making or painting so that he may live a more useful life—able to do so because the local postsecondary institution cares
- the faculty member who, though not under duress to publish, does research that sheds new light on a social or economic problem
- the administrator who takes a leadership role in resolving community problems—and encourages his staff to do likewise

The list can go on and on; it is truly inexhaustible. There are two points to be made. These stories represent public relations opportunities for the institution that are there to be found without much digging. What's more important, these kinds of stories will be readily picked up by the communications media and provide convincing evidence of the impact the college is making on the people of its community.

Beyond the instant visibility inherent in these informational pieces, there is a case and a base for development, for generating public support and assistance for a new program, a new building, additional staff, or better classroom equipment. They provide the evidence needed to convince community leadership of the value of the college and its program. This is where it all starts.

Newspapers, radio, and television will not have the time to look for these stories. Legislators and civic leaders will not know of them. Business leaders cannot take time off from their pursuits to search out examples of college contributions to the economic welfare. If these stories are to be made known and become part of an image of a progressive institution, there must be someone or some office on the campus attuned to the task of bringing them to the attention of the publics which count. No one outside the institution can do it.

It is true that only the positive stories have been hypothesized here, but remember that the thesis of this section has to do with opportunities, not problems. The problem cases will emerge of their own accord: the drug pusher, the malcontent faculty member, the thief. But these will be far fewer in number than those whose lives have been improved by the institution. The latter, if judiciously sought out and programmed into the communications network, will offset the problem cases. That's why it is especially important that the public relations staff not sit back and wait for the problems to arise. Be prepared for them, of course, for they will inevitably come, but they should not be allowed to dictate the style of the program or preoccupy those who must deal with them. Opportunity, therefore, is the watchword of the public relations staff, not problems.

THE NATURE OF THE ACTIVITY

To organize the college relations function, there must be an understanding of what the activity is all about. Since many college authorities have little knowledge of the role of public relations or a very narrow view of what it can and cannot do, one might suggest that they rely on the man or woman they hire to head the office to define it and chart its parameters. This suggestion does not bear careful scrutiny, for how are the authorities to employ an individual who can put together an effective program, if they do not understand the activity in the first place? Some discussion of terminology, objectives, and job descriptions is in order.

Terminology

Public relations people themselves have never been able to settle on one title that covers all aspects of the job, even in the giant corporations that constitute major universities. Terms like public relations, college relations, communications, public information, development, community relations, and public affairs are used interchangeably from campus to campus. The one term that seems to have faded into oblivion is *publicity,* yet, somewhat ironically, that's what most people think of when they hear the term public relations. There is no denying that providing public information continues in importance despite all the high-blown theories and philosophies expounded by thinkers on the subject. The thinkers, it should be noted, are not always the practitioners.

The two most conflicting terms in educational public relations are *public relations* and *development.* For years, the chief operator in the far-flung realm of public relations was called just that—the public relations director (later to become the college, or university, relations director). To him fell a plethora of responsibilities:

- advice and counsel to the president on policy matters relating to the institution's relations with its many publics
- public information or communications with and through the popular media of mass communications
- publications (catalogs, program brochures, annual reports, newsletters) addressed directly to various publics
- fund-raising (later to be elevated and obscured under the term *development*)
- alumni affairs, relating to special efforts to reach former students and graduates
- internal relations, or communications with faculty, students, trustees, advisory groups.

As colleges and universities recognized that financial support would not necessarily be automatically forthcoming, fund raising began to take on new importance. The man or woman who could map a multimillion dollar fund campaign—and succeed in it—seemed logically to fit into the top position. Since raising money depended on a well-grounded public relations program, it seemed appropriate to place responsibility for the combined effort in the person who had the genius for fund raising. The term *fund raising* was not considered a palatable one in the sensitive arena of public relations; it was therefore supplanted by the word *development*, a far more high-sounding title that could be said to include such things as development of learning resources, staff, programs, students, and facilities. Today, universities and colleges continue to show ambiva-

lence toward terminology in this important area. No one
has yet come up with a satisfactory answer to which comes
first—development or public relations. In fact, a new term
has now been coined in education to cover these functions.
The word is *advancement,* which is discussed later in this
chapter. Ideally, what the institution seeks is a person with
a full grasp of and necessary experience in educational
relations who also has genius and expertise at finding
dollars. What title is conferred upon that person is not
exactly the most vital problem facing the institution—
though it may have professional implications for the individual involved.

Public relations and/or development, as will be seen, is
somewhat different in the community college than in the
four-year college or university, but many of the same
principles, the same guidelines, will apply. The techniques
of public relations will be similar no matter what the
nature, the purpose, or the makeup of the institution.

Setting Objectives

A discussion of titles and responsibilities can occupy as
much space as available for it, but there is little to be
gained by engaging in arguments about which comes first or
what title is most important. What is important is to get
the job done, and that brings up the question, What is the
job to be done? How is public or college relations defined?
If it is not merely publicity, if it is not simply fund raising
or development, if it is not just handsome publications,
then what is it? What's the point of it all?

As with the nomenclature for jobs in public relations,
definitions vary from authority to authority and from
institution to institution. No public relations man has ever
found an adequate way to explain what he does for the

benefit of neighbors, children, or his maker. Webster calls
public relations an "art" or "science" and uses terms like
goodwill, interpretative material, reciprocal understanding.
One of the best definitions is that provided by the International Public Relations Association:

> Public relations is a management function, of a continuing and
> planned character, through which public and private organiza-
> tions and institutions seek to win and retain the understanding,
> sympathy, and support of those with whom they are or may be
> concerned—by evaluating public opinion about themselves, in
> order to correlate, as far as possible, their own policies and
> procedures, to achieve by planned and widespread information
> more productive and more efficient fulfillment of their common
> interests.

One part of this definition that is particularly important to
emphasize is that dealing with the question of management:
"Public relations is a management function," because it has
to do with policy making, with the interpretation of policy,
and with the execution of policy. It is not, as is too often
the case, a function to be relegated to some lower-level
echelon of operations not in day-to-day touch with the
pulse of the institution. Public relations is a part of
management. In community college work, in technical
institutes, in other two-year institutions of postsecondary
education, the chief public relations officer should be on
the administrative team.

There are those who might question whether a function
of public relations is to make policy. It is worth questioning. But what is meant here is that this expert, hired for his
special knowledge and skills, would be a part of that
management team involved in the objectives that beget
policies. Michael Radock, vice-president for university relations, the University of Michigan, refers to the policy-

making role of the public relations officer: "The public relations officer plays a policy-making role. How large a role depends not so much on his clearly defined responsibilities as on his colleagues' appreciation of public relations and their willingness to seek and consider professional counsel." This supports my earlier contention that one of the stumbling blocks in the path of good public relations in postsecondary institutions of higher education is lack of understanding and appreciation of the public relations function by those who should rely on it most: the administrators, the trustees, the various governing bodies responsible for the growth and development of the institutions.

Radock also puts forth another term that is being used increasingly in institutional public relations. He suggests that an umbrella title that would embrace all public relations or college relations functions and responsibilities is *advancement,* or advancement programs. Clearly, the notion behind this umbrella term is that ultimately the public relations function is not to extinguish fires but to advance the institution along a variety of fronts, to help it move towards certain well-enunciated goals and concerns. Leading practitioners of educational public relations have embraced the term advancement, some grudgingly. In fact, the former American Alumni Council and the American College Public Relations Association have been reorganized and merged into an organization known as the Council for the Support and Advancement of Education, or CASE.

Nature of the Work

Once a college has set objectives and established policies to attain advancement and progress in carrying out the overall mission (with input from the public relations staff, it is to be hoped) the real work of the administrative unit known as college relations (community relations, public relations, advancement, development, communications) begins. The nature of this work may be illustrated by taking a leaf from the action plan of Carl Byoir & Associates, a major public relations agency:

1. Analysis . . . of policies and objectives of the client . . . of relationships with various publics, including employees, customers, dealers, shareholders, the financial community, government and the press (with continuing research to keep the analysis up-to-date).
2. Planning and programming . . . of specific undertakings and projects in which public relations techniques can be employed to help attain the objectives through effective communication between the client and its publics.
3. Implementation . . . of the programs and projects by maximum and effective use of all avenues of communication, internal and external, to create understanding and stimulate action.

While the above describes the activities of an outside commercial public relations firm, it can readily be adjusted and transposed to describe the job of community college public relations; but the description lacks one activity that I maintain is essential—policy making.

The public relations officer has a role that includes policy making, as suggested by Radock, but once policies are set, the public relations officer begins to look at them in terms of their possible impact on various publics. He or she then begins to plan programs whereby the policies and their possible effects on the people can be interpreted and communicated. Finally, he or she brings into play the most sophisticated techniques to implement the programs. The community college public relations officer should be a part of the college family, yet be able to step back and look with objectivity and perhaps even aloofness at the college program and its potential for advancement. At times, the college may virtually appear to be a client rather than an employer as the public relations officer seeks to bring about the advancement of the institution. He, or she, in short, becomes the inside-outside man or woman of the college—posing such questions as How would this new program look from the standpoint of a leading businessman of the community? What effect will this policy have on the attitude of the chairman of the legislature's committee on education? What will minority groups think of the new admissions plan?—always attempting to stand in the shoes of those whose attitudes may make or break a policy, a program, or a new endeavor.

IN ON THE GROUND FLOOR

The community relations officer, we have established, must operate at a high level if he or she is to be effective. Obviously, the level achieved, the status obtained in any institution will depend upon prevailing attitudes and under-standings of college advancement needs. But a book of this nature can concern itself only with the ideal situation. Certainly programs will vary from institution to institution, based on size, on purpose, on the total organizational outlook, but we can say without equivocation that the public relations officer must be in on the ground floor of institutional advancement. If not, the program may as well be turned over to the president's secretary.

Being in on the ground floor means just that. The

public relations officer ought to be one of the first persons hired in a new institution, perhaps even before it is officially established or opened for business. Colleges just gearing up for this activity must bring new public relations management immediately into the mainstream of decision formulating and execution.

Most colleges today, in a time of change that has caused future shock to take on more than passing meaning, are engaged in institutional soul-searching. They are taking another look at missions developed years ago in the light of new developments, asking whether those missions ought to be renewed and revised. New institutions have an opportunity to develop mission statements on a fresh footing. With the development of new or revised mission statements comes the need for continuing objectives and action plans to insure implementation.

The public relations officer should be an integral part of the team that leads this kind of planning and development. He should have a major role in the process. A mission statement that does not take into account the impact and the implications of the mission upon the variety of audiences to be served will not provide the kind of guidance needed for realization of the purpose of the institution. This is not to imply that one man or woman, schooled and experienced in public relations, can capture in flowing language a noble mission for the institution, nor that other people on the management and advancement team will not be mindful and sensitive to community concerns and aspirations, but public relations expertise ought to be tapped for what it is worth, ought to be brought into play with weight equal to other opinions and ideas.

By way of illustration, take the example of a growing and successful community college in the midwest. It's president says:

When the people of our community decided they wanted a community college, the decision was arrived at after considerable debate, discussion, and study. They had some good ideas about what their community college should be, how it ought to relate to them and to needs, educational and social. One of the first things I did after being appointed president was to staff up in public relations. I knew that we could not translate into an action program what the people wanted without the help of a professional. We got him—and we have placed strong emphasis on that aspect of administration ever since.

This midwestern college, now in existence for seven years, has enjoyed outstanding success and unusual support from the community. The credit does not go, of course, to the public relations program, but it is due to a president, with a supportive board, who saw the need for public relations as a major tool in generating a productive, progressive educational program. The college's public relations program was applauded by a leading local newspaper. Rare, indeed, is it that newspapers publicly acknowledge the usefulness or importance of public relations, despite the fact that the press depends upon the information and ideas that come from public relations people.

So the public relations officer ought to be in on the ground floor, has a role to play in devising the total program—the mission of the institution—then portraying and interpreting it effectively and accurately to the publics for which the college stands. No decision—the locale of a satellite campus or the scheduling of a major speech by the president or the chairman of the board of trustees—is too important to benefit from the counsel of the public relations officer. It should be acknowledged, however, that the public relations officer generally stays in the background. It is not he or she who makes the announcement of a new campus or the establishment of an educational program. He or she may formulate the announcement, plan the timing, determine the means of communication, but it will be the chief administrator, the board chairman, or the head of a faculty committee who will be visible in the communications process.

While the public relations officer has a part in the policy and decision-making process, it is important never to give the appearance that he or she dictates and makes policy irrespective of other elements in the college. Alas, there is still enough suspicion and questioning of the function to make it advisable for the public relations officer to remain in the background, to be called upon only to provide the supplemental information required or to open access to other decision makers in the institution.

IS PUBLIC RELATIONS DIFFERENT IN TWO-YEAR INSTITUTIONS?

Most of the examples of good public relations and the models cited here have come either from the corporate world or from four-year colleges and state universities. The reasons are obvious. Community relations has not been considered a vital function at two-year institutions of postsecondary education, so they provide few models which stand out. The few there are, such as the midwest community college program, will be described, but most of the guidance offered by models must be borrowed from the other segments of higher education.

Radock maintains the job of community relations is different, not only in different kinds of institutions, but from institution to institution, no matter of what kind. Much depends upon the climate of public opinion, the size of the college audience, the mixture of audiences, and the size of the institution itself. But much has been written to suggest that two-year postsecondary institutions are different. They are open-access institutions, reaching out to the many as well as the few. They are characterized by a populism that has not traditionally been associated with higher education. They have variously been called "people's colleges," "democracy's schools," and the "supermarkets" of postsecondary education.

If these institutions are somewhat different, then it stands to reason that their public relations programs ought to be somewhat different, from which it follows that a different outlook will be required of the person who directs the public relations program. As a representative of the people's college, the public relations officer will be required to think of audiences that may be somewhat overlooked on more traditional campuses used to dealing with the elite. He or she will need to be particularly aware of the needs, concerns, and even suspicions of strata of society not previously considered to be college "material": the sons and daughters of blue collar workers and blue collar workers themselves, neglected ethnic groups, the so-called culturally and educationally deprived, poor people of all colors and all backgrounds.

At the same time, it will be necessary to convince people in higher income brackets, men and women in professional work, that they have a leadership role to play in insuring the viability of the community college or technical institute. Many of those citizens who are so needed in "good" causes have no personal experience with two-year institutions of postsecondary education. For many, college is still somewhat exclusive, hardly a place for the masses. It is not so much that many professionals are against two-year postsecondary education for the masses, but that they are passive about a kind of institution they cannot understand. Illustrative of the kind of attitude to be

dealt with is a story told by the president of a junior high
school PTA in a high-income professional suburb of Chicago. He had arranged a monthly PTA meeting around
school counseling. Calling together the program committee,
he suggested that a panel be gotten together that would
include a high school counselor, a university counselor, and
a representative of the county community college. One of
the members of the committee said, "I think the program
is a good one. But why have anyone from the community
college? It is not likely that our sons and daughters will be
going to that school." Such snobbishness is breaking down
of its own accord, mainly because more and more young
people are opting for two-year institutions in their own
communities, even those from the "better" families, but
that attitude persists and will continue to be a problem for
most public relations officers as they set sights and objectives on the total public relations program.

One area in which the attitudes of professionals toward
the education represented by two-year institutions can most
hurt the efforts of the public relations officer is that of the
mass media. By and large, most journalists and broadcasters
come from four-year college and university backgrounds,
particularly those who handle the education beat. They can
write, report, and discover positive stories in connection
with higher education as they know it—that which is
represented by four-year colleges and universities. They
know what goes on on the college or university campus.
But the community college is not within the realm of their
first-hand knowledge and experience. Frankly, they tend to
look down on institutions with programs of less than four
years not leading to baccalaureate degrees. Such institutions
are not a part of their experience.

That, too, will change as time goes on, as the journalism field begins to employ persons whose postsecondary

educational experience may have started in community colleges, technical institutes, or even proprietary schools and colleges. Until it does, however, this built-in attitude will be a constant stumbling block for community college communicators. It will make their jobs far more difficult than that of their counterparts on the campuses of other types of colleges and universities.

As previously indicated, the community college public relations officer must take into account audiences that are new to higher education and find new ways to overcome suspicion and distrust, if not open hostility, on the part of some groups. By the same token, the community college public relations officer must deal with an ironic fact: some of the community college's very reasons for being, some of its strongest appeals and attractions, are by their very nature negative factors in the American outlook on what is good and not good in society. It is not just a matter of class, though that is a solid factor. Being from an Ivy League college has always been "better" than being a graduate of a major state university; matriculation at a state university has always been more esteemed than matriculation at a state college; and so on. See where that puts the community college. Aside from that, however, the community college, the technical institute, the two-year proprietary institution does the unthinkable. It takes in people who have not even completed high school, much less achieved average scholastic standings. It does not have dormitories; people have to commute. Therefore, without a large resident body, there can't be much social or cultural life. It offers vocational training—programs for hard hats. It offers a degree—but what does an associate degree mean in the marketplace? A huge percentage of students on two-year campuses work part time. What kind of a college scene does that make for? On the face of it, these would appear to be largely negative aspects of the community college image. That is why for years it bore such sobriquets as dumping ground, second-chance university, and tinker-toy tech.

The fact is, for the public relations officer of such a postsecondary institution, this is the real story. These and other somewhat negative spokes make up the wheel of the community college story. If the public relations officer derogates these factors or becomes defensive about them, then he is not telling the real story. So he has a different kind of public relations problem—turning the negative into the positive.

Historically, the two-year institutions of postsecondary education have been defensive about their roles. Many have tended to downplay the true virtues of the institution—its great mix of people and programs—and play up the academic side, to ape their four-year counterparts. This, of course, has not worked and will not work. Recent changes in society, in attitudes toward education and toward the world of work, have clearly shown that the public does not want more Ivy League institutions or massive new universities; they cannot make use of all that now exist. The two-year institution has come into its own, possibly despite itself.

The community college has not eliminated the negative; it has instead turned the negative into positive at a time when something new, something different, something appealing is needed in American education. For the public relations man or woman, it provides an opportunity and a challenge that is to be sought after. The job is different from those to be found in other educational institutions. It will often mean charting one's own course in waters not charted before. With proper backup and administrative support, the position provides the opportunity to try new approaches, to be creative, and to have a significant voice in the affairs of the institution.

Guidelines for Chapter 2 ———————————

In this chapter, some of the elements that go into the making of a good public relations program in a community college have been discussed. Creating that good program, making it work, must take place in an atmosphere of understanding of current thinking in the field in general, of attitudes toward the professional function, and of its place in the management hierarchy. Here are some guidelines for planning:

1. The view of the public relations activity in the two-year institution of postsecondary education must be broadened from that of a narrow public information function to a far-reaching program supporting through many mechanisms the purposes of the institution.
2. Rather than consider public relations as principally a matter of problem solving, it should be emphasized that it is essentially a matter of taking advantage of opportunities to present the college in the best possible light.
3. There's a confusion of titles for the public relations function. In general, the best term in the two-year institution is that of community relations. This may encompass public information, publications, fund

raising (development), speakers' bureaus, and special events.

4. Public relations is a management function. The position must not be relegated to a low-level status if it is to be carried out effectively.

5. The public relations officer is best placed in a policy-making position and certainly has a role in helping to carry out and interpret policy.

6. The public relations officer should be in on the ground floor of establishment and development of an institution, where his or her counsel will be vital.

7. Public relations is different in the community-based postsecondary institution—particularly in audiences to be reached—and that must be considered in staffing and organizing.

8. The public relations officer must turn the negative into the positive.

9. Institutions of postsecondary education should exchange information and ideas on to public relations planning. They should study and adapt to their own programs elements of tried and tested programs in other institutions that seem to fit. At the same time, community, junior, and technical colleges have the opportunity to innovate in building advancement activities.

Integrating
the Parts _____ 3

"I am looking for a course that will prepare me for real estate selling," the student said to his counselor. "I want to take it up as a sideline in order to help pay my way through college."

"Fine," the counselor replied, "but why not try the catalog. I am sure you can find out whether the course is going to be offered next semester."

"Well, I took one look at that thing and I just threw it down," the student said sheepishly. "There's a real estate course offered, but I can't tell whether it is available to me—you know I am in history—or whether it's strictly for business types. That catalog is just too much!"

"Well, let's take another look at it," the counselor said, knowing that she, too, would find it difficult to figure out the answer. She had received more complaints about the catalog than any other publication or activity of the college.

In this situation, the public relations office had no input into the college catalog. Yet, here is a publication that is seen by more people and referred to by more would-be students than perhaps any other piece of literature issued by the institution. First impressions of a college are often formed as a result of the college catalog. It is, depending upon one's perspective, the Good Book or the Bad Book of the institution. Far too frequently, it is poorly organized; the type is so small as to be unreadable; and it is full of contradictions. There is a long-standing debate about college catalogs, who organizes them, how,

and when. I do not intend to go into that debate here. The
anecdote with which this chapter begins illustrates the
essential need to integrate the various parts of the public
relations message and functions into a working, workable
whole. The catalog, since it is the first point-of-contact for
many who will be taking advantage of postsecondary
opportunities, is a good starting point to substantiate the
need for integrating the public relations program.

If it can be assumed that the typical community-based
college or school intends to project the image of an
accessible, open, appealing institution, then it is obvious
that the catalog, the device used most frequently by those
who would enter the college, should somehow or other
encompass that message. It should make things easier—not
more difficult— for the potential client. Obviously, the
college relations office cannot be expected to plan the
course schedule and to decide what is to be offered when.
But that office can, because of its expertise and understanding of communications, provide assistance to those
responsible for the college program. It can prepare, in
consultation with appropriate authorities, the general message and introductory remarks about the college. It can
advise on how to organize the book so as to make it
readable and understandable. It can plan the graphics for
the book to make it appealing and even exciting. That is a
good start on the road to building and implementing a
good program of public relations for the institution. It
follows, then, that almost everything, if not everything,
that smacks of communication about the institution, should
bear the imprint of the college relations experts—from the
most innocuous press release to the dedication speech and
to the college catalog.

While the college catalog serves as a good example of an
important formal beginning point for the public relations

program, one could step back even a bit more to activities which precede issuance of that important document. When a potential student telephoned to request the catalog, how was the call handled? In a pleasant, helpful way? Or nonchalantly and haphazardly? Or, if the request came by letter, was there a reply? Was the book sent promptly? Was the person encouraged to visit the campus and get better acquainted? The point is that we are dealing with a total, integrated program of college relations. A program that eventually involves every employee, every volunteer worker, every student, everyone who represents the institution in any capacity whatsoever. In this chapter, however, we will deal with the more formal aspects of the public relations office and functions.

WHAT ARE THE PARTS?

Up until now, we have talked about public relations, or college relations, in a very general way. I hope it has become clear to the nonpractitioner and been reaffirmed for the practitioner that the public relations function is a somewhat complex, demanding, and challenging activity on any institution's campus. Publicity, as we have stated, is the image many persons apply to public relations, and many college public relations practitioners continue to feed that image by acting more like press agents than public relations professionals. When such "press agents" spotlight college beauty queens, athletes, and contrived gags, the college is not helped. A picture of a pretty girl celebrating the end of exams by throwing her books and legs into the air tells little about the meaning and purpose of higher education. Publicity can serve a purpose, of course, if it can help win the total public relations battle. I recall an incident connected with my first college relations job that makes the point. Eager and excited and bent on getting the best possible local coverage for the institution's program, I was soon at a loss to understand why the morning newspaper in the local community, the paper with the largest circulation, either didn't use or down played all the releases I delivered to them. The city editor, a crotchety gentleman of the old school of journalism, who usually treated me with great disdain, one night gave me a clue toward solving the morning newspaper dilemma. On delivering a release about the upcoming college commencement to him personally, a practice I always followed in my eagerness to please, he looked at me and growled, "Don't you have some good looking girls up at that college?"

It so happened that within a few days we did have a beauty contest, the kind of event we normally downplayed. But I managed to get a picture of the women in modestly revealing shorts and hustled it off to the morning paper. The next day that picture appeared two-column on page one, and from that day forward, stories from the college got better and bigger play in that newspaper, and I never forgot that the city editor liked to look at pretty young women. That is perhaps a form of press agentry and of male chauvinism. It was used only as a means, however, to fulfill a larger purpose, not to create an image of the institution as a mecca for beauty queens.

A large corporation used to tell its new public relations employees that it was concerned with the larger picture of the company, not just with newspaper space or magazine spreads, but the man who could get a two-page spread in one of the national magazines was the first man to get a promotion and a fat bonus. So publicity is one part of the public relations program. If one were to list all the parts, the grouping would come out about as follows, with variations from institution to institution.

1. *Management*: This essential part of the job concerns two aspects of the function. It deals with management of the institution, and the part that public relations plays in that management in terms of policy making and policy interpretation and implementation. It also deals with the fairly sizeable job, depending upon the situation, of administering a department of the school or college. Budgets, time, and personnel must be managed effectively in order to insure a responsive and productive program of public relations.

2. *Public relations counsel*: Perhaps this part could be lumped under the heading of management, although it is separated out here because of the almost personal, special nature of the activity. It includes advice and assistance that the public relations person may be able to provide, not only on the conduct of the institution, but also on the personal conduct and actions of chief administrators and perhaps board members. Is it appropriate, for example, for the president to accept an assignment with some fact-finding commission or international study group that will take him away from the campus for a long period of time? If judged appropriate, how should the circumstance be interpreted to the community?

3. *Public information*: Usually, this part of the organized public relations effort is defined as relations or dealings with the media—newspapers, radio and television, magazines, and various community organs such as the Chamber of Commerce newsletter or magazine. The communications media represent the fastest channels for disseminating the college message to large audiences, dealing with them is obviously a

vital and sensitive part of the whole, for what appears in the public prints or on the airwaves cannot be easily undone. Public information is a daily, programmed activity which requires understanding of the technical nature of the media as well as the thirst of journalists for that which is different, new, exciting—and perhaps controversial and sensational.

4. *Publications*: As differentiated from public information, although closely tied to that part, publications constitute a means whereby the institution presents its message or messages in a form which it thinks portrays the college, the program, or the activity being described in the best, most accurate and appealing way. Apart from what the publication may say, it can be packaged in such a way as to present an image of a lively, imaginative, innovative institution. Included among publications would be program brochures, catalogs, annual reports, community newsletters, form letters conveying policy announcements, and calendars of public events and activities.

5. *Public speeches*: An effective means of disseminating information about such things as important policy changes, new policies, or responses to criticisms of some college activity or program is speeches or pronouncements by chief administrators or the chairman of the board. The public relations officer is called upon to provide input in two ways. First, he or she may help to draft the speech, announcement, or pronouncement for the person who may deliver it. Second, he or she will assist in determining an appropriate time, place, and event for issuing the statement in order to get the best possible coverage for it. Some questions the public relations officer

will need to answer are: Should the speech be given
before a college meeting or a town meeting? Should
it be delivered at a meeting of an important civic
group? Is the address timed so that it will provide
the best opportunity for press coverage—prior to
deadlines of the most important media?

6. *Speakers' bureau*: One of the best ways to inculcate
a feeling of support and interest in an institution is
to expose the knowledge and expertise of individuals
among faculty and administrators. These people constitute a ready-made resource for public relations
and community service. Opportunity found, possibly
in a formal manner, such as via a speakers' bureau,
for faculty to appear on programs where they can
talk about their particular fields of endeavor. It
should be noted that in such an activity it is
information and knowledge about the particular individual's discipline, avocation, or special interest that
is imparted, not the official posture of the college.
(In addition to scheduling faculty for formal program slots at meetings of community groups, arrangements should be made to use these individuals in
connection with news stories dealing with important
local, state, regional, or national events. For
example, if NASA sends up a moon shot, the event
can be localized with some timely comments from
the college's leading science teachers. Or if the White
House issues a statement on the economy, the
institution's resident economics expert can talk
about what it will mean for the local community.
These are contrived but useful techniques for offering service and public relations contributions.)

7. *Special events*: Dedications, commencements, ground
breakings, inaugurals are traditions in America. While

there are many who today derogate the relevance of
such events to the needs of today's society, the fact
is that people do cling to them and seem to expect
them, so they continue to constitute an important
means of gaining attention for postsecondary educational institutions. In fact, in some ways, these
events have even more meaning for constituents of
community-based institutions, many of whom —the
families, the friends, the supporters of the institution—might not otherwise experience the college
feeling. Though the public relations office does not
normally generate these kinds of events, it does
concern itself with scheduling, timing, formats, and
perhaps the drafting of speeches and remarks that
may be presented.

8. *Cultural and entertainment spectacles*: The community college, if truly responsive to community needs,
will provide the facilities, the place, for cultural and
entertainment attractions for its family of supporters. In many communities, the college or school may
be the only appropriate place for a concert, a play,
or a lecture. It may also be called upon to provide
for such controversial events as rock festivals and
politically related demonstrations. The public relations office, while again not necessarily in a position
to create such spectaculars, will have a vital role in
advising on whether certain groups should appear or
whether certain activities should be conducted, on
timing, and on advance promotion. In the case of
some functions, such as rock festivals or peaceful
demonstrations, the college public relations office
will be in close touch with media and perhaps even
with enforcement authorities to assure appropriate
communication, about happenings surrounding the
event, as well as about the event itself.

9. *Alumni relations*: Two-year institutions of post-secondary education have tended to overlook or bypass formal programs involving alumni on the assumptions that transfers will have loyalty to the institution from which they receive baccalaureate degrees and that two-year graduates who go into employment upon completion will neither be in a position nor have the inclination to contribute in any tangible way to the welfare of the institution. Such thinking is erroneous and, very fortunately, changing. A spirit of loyalty can be engendered among those who will and do transfer. Those who take jobs in the community will be the voters and the ongoing supporters of the institution. But special attention is required to obtain the proper spirit of support and cooperation; that will be a part of the total public relations assignment.

10. *Employee relations*: As a later chapter will show, the public relations activity involves everyone in the insititution. It is essential that college employees be fully informed and have complete understanding of actions and activities of the institute. It will usually be the responsibility of the public relations officer to insure effective communication among employees. Various devices will be used—newsletters; presidential memoranda; frequent informal meetings to discuss new policies and programs; the use of faculty, students, and others on public relations committees; the involvement of employees in fund campaigns and other programs. If the employee, who is close to what is going on, does not understand what is happening, then it is not likely that other publics will find it easy to comprehend campus situations and the prevailing atmosphere. Lack of understanding on the part of employees

may lead to problems far more difficult than the effort to insure proper communication and open channels for dialog.

11. *Development (fund raising)*: Come to be considered a special art in post-secondary education, fund raising is just beginning to come into its own as a necessary function in community-based institutions that are organized on a two-year basis. Until recently, it was generally consigned to a financial-aide officer or a dean of student personnel and limited to the raising of support from government-financed programs. Often, it has had little or no tie with public relations. But, as emphasized before, fund raising depends upon a good and effective public relations program to achieve the desired objectives. The office of development, working under the public relations umbrella, should incorporate private solicitation as well as procurement of government grants.

One other part that deserves special treatment but might be categorized under one or more of the above, and will certainly involve all of the above, is the special campaign for example, the drive to pass a special bond issue, the multimillion dollar fund campaign, an effort to launch a controversial new curriculum. The functions could be broken down further. However, these are the major parts that most community colleges would want to consider, and in any one of those activities, one might find still other pieces to fit into the puzzle of public relations. These parts are not necessarily broken down into descending order of importance, for at some institutions, the last might well come first, but I believe that, if a solid program is built on the other fronts, fund raising will certainly have greater prospects for success.

PUTTING THE PARTS TOGETHER

How do these parts and pieces go together to make up the total public relations program? Is there any rhyme or reason to the program? How are all these parts coordinated? Obviously, not all the parts will come into play for each college circumstance or situation that involves public relations, but it is safe to say that most major policy changes, new policies, or major decisions will use, or take advantage of, the techniques, functions, and activities described here. That is, all the parts of the public relations program should be used to advantage in creating the kind of image and public perspective that is desired.

To illustrate, let us take a hypothetical situation that will undoubtedly arise in most postsecondary institutions at one time or another and that will bring into play most of the parts we have discussed. The college's mission calls for eventual outreach of facilities and program into all geographic sections of the community. The college now has one major campus; its plan calls for the establishment of two more, which would presumably make facilities geographically accessible to all sectors. Studies have been made of the needs, and approximate locations of the two remaining campuses have been selected. The question that faces the college authorities and its board is which of the two locations will be built first, recognizing that only one can be established for the foreseeable future. The earlier plan, designating a three-step plan of action, had been accepted, but years have gone by and the community has new political leadership. Times, in short, have changed since the earlier decision was made. A new look has to be taken;

possibly a new decision should be made on the location of a second campus.

Using this illustration, we can see how public relations is involved from the time the new decision is made until the campus is actually dedicated. For our purposes here, we will telescope a normal time span into one year. Keep in mind that the new decision is more or less irrevocable. The public relations job is to condition and prepare the way for creation and establishment of the new campus. We will not get involved here in possible controversy or conflict with regard to the decision, although that might occur under some circumstances.

So here we are at the time of decision. The public relations man is involved in the final board meeting dealing with the subject. He has, of course, provided the other college management people, as well as the board, with background material, particularly as regards public opinion, media support, likely conflicts, and possible opposition. Acting on information gathered, he has made his recommendation with regard to the site, in this case making a positive recommendation. His role in this meeting is a dual one: to present his final advice and counsel as the board prepares to take a vote and, after the vote, to convey and interpret the decision to the public through the communications media. He may carry out the latter responsibility by arranging and staging a press conference following the meeting and by providing information for press releases and information kits during the year ahead.

Following the release of the announcement, the public relations office will begin a series of releases dealing with various aspects of carrying out the new campus plan. The campaign will include backgrounders on reaction of the people in the section where the satellite is to be established, programs to be offered and how they will meet particular needs, construction progress, financing progress (although basic financing obviously will have been arranged prior to the decision), and interviews with potential users.

The public relations office will plan a program of addresses by key college officials and board members dealing with the ramifications of the project and what the new branch will do for the community. Such speeches will be programmed for civic and business groups. At the same time, fund-raising activities will be set in motion. Assuming that basic funding is already available, these activities will concentrate on special programs for which support may be obtained from federal or state agencies, on procurement of equipment and financial assistance from corporations in the community, and on possible proposals to national foundations for support of innovative activities beyond the normal or formal program of education.

Meanwhile, a new college catalog will be in preparation. The public relations office will design and plan program brochures to issue prior to the offical opening of the campus and months before the first student arrives. It will publish special direct mail materials to send to various community groups that will be affected by the satellite.

As a special event, a major celebration will be planned for groundbreaking. Civic and state leaders will be involved. The event will provide the stage and the occasion for a major state-of-the-college address by the president or the chairman of the board of directors. A committee will be formed to plan still another major event for the opening of the campus. As a precursor to the opening, the site will become the setting for an outdoor concert or a sports program. The intent from the outset will be to present this campus as a community resource, a place for the people.

Recognizing that some faculty and staff will be diverted to the new campus, communications addressed to employees will give reports on the progress of the program. The faculty's need to know will be great; curiosity will be high; understanding will be vital.

Utilizing the speakers' bureau, faculty will be invited to speak, on subjects that they will be teaching, to meetings of groups in the new sector. Every effort will be made to acquaint citizens with those who will be teaching.

It should be clear from the chart of public relations flow that most of the tools and talents of the public relations office are integrated and brought into play in any large, all-encompassing effort of the institution to improve or advance itself. In this hypothetical case, drawn from discussions with and observations of many top public relations people in both educational and corporate public relations, it is obvious that very little is done without some consideration of the impact on the perceptions of the institution by publics and people. Without any staff or plan, much the same would be done, but too often in such a disorganized and haphazard way as to impede rather than promote progress. It is also obvious that much of the public relations effort could well be put under the heading of accountability, that much overworked but still useful tool of modern-day administrative leadership and management.

In every institution, the approach used in our hypothetical case might be altered or modified to suit understandings and perceptions of the community. For example, community-based educational institutions, in their efforts to be innovative and with it in today's society, are following the lead of many of their own students who scorn tradition and scoff at the ornate and ostentatious. Dedications and groundbreaking ceremonies, like commencements, may give way to more free-spirited, less well-planned celebrations that are calculated to draw attention without the trappings that once were considered essential in higher education.

PUBLIC RELATIONS PROGRAM FOR NEW SITE

Policy Making

1. Public relations officer: Contributes to decision to proceed on second campus
2. provides plan of action for public relations

Public Information

1. Public relations officer: Releases report on decision
2. arranges press conference
3. Public relations office issues: backgrounders periodically during the year
4. announcements of construction progress
5. releases on programs to be offered

Public Speeches

1. President gives backgrounder at important community meeting
2. New dean describes program at educational conference
3. Chairman gives midyear progress report
4. President announces opening—gives dedication address

Special Events

1. Ground-breaking ceremony
2. Community event at half-way point of project
3. Dedication ceremony

Speakers' Bureau

Faculty and other staff give addresses throughout the year to acquaint community groups with specialties that will be offered

Advice and Counsel

President and other authorities, through frequent conferences, are advised on problems and conflicts that have come up and how to cope with them

Fund Raising

1. Campaign charted to raise program support
2. Goals announced
3. Volunteers involved
4. Proposals prepared; calls made

Publications

1. Catalog prepared
2. Program brochures issued
3. Direct mail pieces outlining admissions procedures issued
4. A modest newsletter developed to inform citizens of plans and progress

Of course there may also be some missing ingredients in the public relations program for the new site. There may be some parts of the puzzle that could be eliminated or that do not help to create the picture that is desired. But the point is that a program, a plan, is needed. Some sense of continuity must be built into the public relations program as it supports and and supplements the mission and goals of the institution, whether in terms of a short-range activity, such as the one cited here, or in terms of the long-range goals of the institution. The first, in effect, supports and complements the latter.

PROGRAMS AND PLANS

In addition to showing how the parts of the public relations program fit into the whole, the previous section also illustrates why public relations, like the total institution with its divisions and parts, should have a stated, well-documented program or plan of action to guide staff in carrying out their work. For too many years, educational institutions somehow or other stumbled forward without solid planning and with little attention to the future, to the possibility that there might be changing attitudes toward the college degree and/or professional achievement. Lack of planning was cloaked in the mantle of academic freedom, which too often merely meant poor management. The public relations activity tended to be run on a sort of emergency basis, with far too much time given over to crisis situations. But the scene has changed. Some colleges have found the institution itself at stake. College people no longer are necessarily considered the elite of society. Some colleges have disappeared from the scene with little or no lament from any but those who suddenly found themselves without jobs.

In these new times, the mission of the public relations office will be to help insure that the mission of the institution itself is carried forward. The term mission implies a kind of crusading, evangelizing process, but even a negative mission requires the tools, talents, and techniques of public relations. For example, assume that the authorities of some farsighted college see handwriting on the wall that indelibly indicates that the institution must go out of business within a given time. There is no prospect for saving the college. A good deal of sensitive, intelligent public relations is needed to pave the way for such a happening, to soften the blow to students, to teachers who will be displaced, to alumni who love the institution, to supporters who have kept the institution in operation. Though that kind of assignment will not fall to many public relations people, it is essential that good public relations plans and programs be available to cover whatever circumstance in which the institution might find itself.

The college has a mission. The public relations office examines that mission, builds its long-term programs and plans around it, and provides some of the essential ingredients for its realization, assisting the college in avoiding pitfalls, communicating its desirable and positive features to its many publics, meeting problems and crises with intelligence and understanding. In addition, the public relations office may construct several short-term programs that will support continuing objectives within the mission and meet more specific short-term objectives that relate to the job.

For example, once the institution has decided that to carry out its mission, the public relations office must assure a constant flow of information to the local press and good coverage of the institution by all the media. This is a continuing objective. During a given time, under that continuing objective, the office will want to have at least

six major institutional stories covered by the local newspapers, a weekly discussion show on the major television
station, and a publication about the institution that will be
widely distributed in the community through schools,
libraries, and community agencies. These are specific objectives. As a part of the continuing objective, the office will
also make input into overall institutional planning by
showing that the public information program is vital to the
mission.

    Plans of action are necessary to insure that the objec-
tives are realized. Each plan of action should deal with a
very specific activity. Each should serve as a constant
reminder to those involved in the process that there is a job
to be done, and each should also serve as a timetable which,
as action is checked off, will show progress, success, failure,
or delay. The plan shows exactly how the staff will go
about the job and how responsibilities are distributed. It
reflects dates or projections of dates when certain aspects
of the job are to be accomplished. A typical action plan
would look something like this:

THE PLAN: Arrange for broadcast of a weekly discussion show
dealing with college programs on Station XYZ, April 1 to April 1.

Steps	Due Date	Responsibility
1. Create a program concept, giv- ing titles and ingredients of at least three programs	Sept. 1	PR staff with help of faculty who might participate
2. Initial letter to the station requesting a hearing on the project	Aug. 10	President
3. Meeting with station officials to offer tentative idea	Aug. 20	President, PR chief, dean

---

4. Go ahead to come up with program, given by station	Aug. 25	
5. Meeting arranged with program staff of station to present concept	Sept. 15	Station staff and college PR staff
6. Plan modified according to station's needs	Sept. 20	PR staff
7. New concept with station's needs reflected	Oct. 20	PR staff
8. College representatives who will appear on the show meet	Nov. 12	PR staff
9. Work continues on format, concept	Dec. 1	PR staff
10. Arrangements made for pilot show	Jan. 15	All principals and PR staff
11. Pilot show reviewed and edited	Jan. 30	All principals
12. Series begins	Feb. 15	
13. Advance publicity prepared and program of publicity for duration of show worked out	Feb. 1	PR staff with station reps

This plan is simple. Putting it on paper and including the roles of those who will make it go—from president to dean, to other college representatives and station executives—helps to create a sense of commitment by all concerned. The action plan becomes an official document held by a number of people who recognize that its workability, its coming to fruition, depends upon them. This kind of plan has a disciplinary effect. It represents a means of organizing for a job that has been recognized as essential to the implementation of the institution's mission. It should be kept in mind, too, that the college or community relations log book will contain a number of plans dealing

with other aspects of the program, so time and energy must
be parceled out in a number of directions. Having concrete
plans on paper to which to refer will insure that each plan
receives appropriate attention and gets necessary priority.

The sample plan raises some other points. The chief
administrator has been used sparingly. In an average-sized
community, to get a series of discussion programs on the
major television station is no mean accomplishment and
may require some pull that the public relations man alone
does not have. Thus, the president is brought into the act
in the initial stages. Presumably, if he is the kind of civic
leader that he should be, he will have a personal acquaint-
anceship with the head of the station. He will use that
relationship only in the sense that he can go right to the
top without being unknown. His appeal will not be on the
basis of friendship nor on the basis that the station has an
obligation to engage in this kind of programming; it will be
on the basis that the college is willing to make a contribution to the communications medium and that the station
will have an opportunity to communicate worthwhile pub-
lic-service programming to the viewers. Of course the
president will not demand instant acceptance of the idea;
that's why the term *hearing* was used in the plan. He asks
only for the college to be heard, in terms of the offering
that is being made to the station. Once the initital steps
involving the president have been covered, then the public
relations office must show its talent, its ability to create an
idea and put together a program that will compete favorably with all other public institutions that want to get on
the air in the fierce competition of broadcasting.

Finally, the plan of action makes it possible for the
public relations chief, or the chief administrator, to know
what is going on, what activities are being charted, and
whether they are being accomplished. It is another tool of

accountability, not meant to be an axe hanging over the heads of personnel but to keep management cognizant and informed of planning and development. The well-organized public relations office, therefore, will follow the latest management techniques in programming and planning to help the institution work toward its mission in the best possible climate of support and public interest. Without such an effort, even if the college has the most talented staff in the world, the public relations program will stumble and stammer from lack of coordination with other members of the college team.

The public relations program that lacks focus, that is catch-as-catch-can, will do little to contribute to the good of the institution. If the only plan is to get publicity for board members, or to publicize local athletic contests, then it is not a plan. There is much at stake. Many public relations men and women still come from the world of journalism, as a later chapter will show. As creative people, they may tend not to be as organized and orderly as administrators in some other departments, but there are many opportunities for training and professional development in management. Those opportunities should be made available to the public relations staff.

Guidelines for Chapter 3 ⸻⸻⸻⸻

In this chapter, the many parts of public relations have been described, as well as the way all the parts come together to make up a picture, albeit somewhat of a puzzle, of how and why a good program works. Here are some guidelines:

1. Even those things which are often considered minor and perhaps not deserving of public relations attention, such as the catalog, are a part of the public relations picture.
2. Do not overemphasize publicity for publicity's sake.
3. A good public relations program will include at least these parts: management, public relations counsel, public information, publications, public speeches, speakers' bureaus, special events, cultural and entertainment spectaculars, alumni relations, employee relations, development (fund raising).
4. All of these parts should be programmed to help the institution to carry out major policy decisions that relate to its mission.
5. A good public relations program will have short-term and long-term plans for implementing the total college program on behalf of the mission.

6. Action plans should provide a step-by-step account of how to get the job done.
7. The president and other top administrators should be involved only sparingly in most action planning.
8. An action plan serves as a management tool as well as a guide to getting the job done.
9. Planning and programming is a constant, ongoing activity in itself.

Organization and Staff _____4

"We simply cannot afford to bring high-priced public relations talent to our staff," said the concerned president at a workshop on public relations and development. "We need more resources for our library—and we don't even know where the money for that project is coming from." "That's true," another participant echoed him, "I understand that public relations talent comes high. There are a lot of other things on my campus that have to be considered first."

"Did you ever stop to think that maybe, with the right public relations team and a good program, you might stand a much better chance of getting the other resources you need?" a public relations man responded to the two presidents. "Maybe you have to look on the expenditure of funds for this kind of work as risk capital. It's a gamble that is worth the plunge, and more likely than not, will pay for itself—and many other college needs—many times over if staff are given enough time and freedom."

The questions raised by the administrators at the workshop are recurring ones. Probably in no other field is it more difficult to justify expenditure of necessary funds to establish and maintain a good public relations program. It is not academic; it is not vocational; it doesn't teach or bring about learning; it doesn't, in the eyes of many, add anything to the substance of the college program. But if you look at the more successful colleges, both two-year and four-year, public and private, you will more often than not find a strong and aggressive public relations and development operation.

That the debate goes on in the community college sector is due to the relative "newness" of the institution and the fact that many of the colleges either were directly appended to public school systems or modeled their administrative structures after secondary schools. The superintendent of schools was often the public relations executive, and it followed that the president of a community college would take on that responsibility as well. (In California, many chiefs of community colleges still retain the combined title of superintendent-president, where they are responsible for multicampus districts.) The debate will probably continue, but there are growing signs that the function has been accepted, although many colleges may not yet know how to fit it in, what kind of talent should be recruited, and what charges should be given the staff.

That the picture is changing is supported by a study by Maynard F. Jensen in 1973 of community college public relations programs in Oregon and Washington.

The 1973 survey indicated that 19 PR directors (86 percent) hold administrative rank at their institutions, one director (5 percent) holds faculty rank, while two directors failed to answer the question (of rank). Nineteen (86 percent) of directors report directly to their presidents, while two do not and one did not answer. In the matter of being kept informed of administrative matters, 91 percent answered favorably, as compared to an 86 percent favorable response two years earlier.

Both Oregon and Washington have advanced very rapidly in recent years in community college development. And both states can boast of community college systems that enjoy good public relations.

Jensen is not satisfied, however, with the level of public relations activity among the community colleges of Oregon and Washington.

> The public relations programs at the community colleges in Washington and Oregon, taken as a whole, are not well developed. . . . Substantiation of the hypothesis was bolstered by the lack, in many instances, of separate public relations departments, by lack of staffing with qualified directors and assistants, by limited budgetry resources, and by a tenuous grasp of the significance of professional public relations programs on the part of a number of college administrators. The majority of PR directors did not perceive their roles as those of providing complete public relations services, failed to be fully aware of their institutions' varied publics and, in the rare instances where public opinion was sampled, did not make the best possible use of the information obtained.

It could be said that no public relations man is ever satisfied with the amount of money he has to spend, the latitude he has in developing new programs, or the kind of support staff that may be available to him. But neither is the director of auto mechanics or the business department or the maintenance section. That's the name of the game in today's Parkinsonian world. It is not likely, however, that the problem of riches will be a major one for public relations departments of community colleges for a long time to come. They will continue to struggle for enough support to conduct a meaningful, effective, and progressive program, which is what this chapter is all about.

WHERE DOES THE INSTITUTION START?

As we have seen in the preceding chapter, there are many functions to be performed in a good and effective public relations program. In fact, the administrator who penetrates this book may be dismayed and disillusioned as he reviews the parts that go into the whole of public relations. He may well ask himself: Do we need a specialist for each of these areas? How could one possibly afford that kind of effort?

Fortunately, while there may be exceptions to the rule, the parts do not represent bodies. They represent the things that need to be done, the bases that must be covered if the activity is to be effective. If there is a superman or superwoman available to do them all, then hire that person at any price. That may sound facetious, but the fact is that there are many well-rounded professionals in public relations who do have the expertise in all the areas—publications, public information, management, special events, etc.— who could, if forced to, accept the challenge and perform a one-person service encompassing many of the parts. Unfortunately, time and energy are factors.

In starting and staffing the program, however, certain assumptions must be made. They can be catalogued as follows:

Assumption 1: In order to effectively carry out its mission, the college needs public relations support.

Assumption 2: Budgetary means will be made available to institute such a program.

Assumption 3: Public relations will be considered a high-level function with a management role in the total administrative operation.

Assumption 4: Accorded that kind of prominence, it follows that a person with competence

and understanding and professional experience should be made responsible for
input into development of a program.

Assumption 5: The college will need to engage in an
intensive, careful recruiting effort to
obtain the kind of person needed.

An overall assumption must also be made that the
institution is starting from scratch, that it is in effect
beginning anew in the field of public relations. However, a
college that already has a program in progress, perhaps with
minimal staff, should look at how that effort can be
buttressed and improved. If there is a director or chief
officer of public relations already on board, then he or she
should be given opportunity to make inputs before any
changes are made. The point is that a logical beginning is to
get someone to head up the program, to help create it, to
breathe some life into it. Then provide the necessary
support for that person to create the program.

Colleges that have access to management counseling
services or planning consultants may choose to take that
route. Certainly, such services are retained and used in
planning facilities and curriculums and in developing long-
range goals. Essentially, however, such consultants will offer
advice along lines similar to what is being provided here:
that the college may have an idea of the kind of program
in which it hopes to engage, that the public relations
counsel may help to develop that program, but that the
program cannot take firm shape and must be left flexible
enough to allow for a top-flight director to give it the
momentum and scope required.

So the place to start is with an assumption that a
program is needed; some broad outlines have been set

forth. In an institution just being formed, the public relations officer may be one of the first persons hired after the institution has started. In a college that has been in operation, with only minimal public relations services offered, a new public relations effort will require recruitment of the right person to head up the program.

THE RIGHT PERSON

Qualifications

Only seers and soothsayers could predict and readily engage the "right person." All the pedigrees and experience in the world would not necessarily translate to community college settings. But what people have to go on are what appears on paper, on résumés, the kinds of experiences the individual has had, the sort of recommendations they receive, and the personal appearance and attitudes they bring with them to the job. Appearance and attitudes are particularly sensitive in public relations, and especially so in the community college. Writing experience, editing knowhow, and management prowess may not offset the kind of personality that turns people off.

Incidentally, the public relations chief should have at least a bachelor's degree, possibly a master's. If he or she has a doctorate, in combination with appropriate experience, there may be some added potential for good relations with the educational community. Whether we like it or not, this person must be working in an educational setting where proper credentials are important.

The president of a large, midwestern university, interviewing a woman to head up the public relations program of the institution, was very candid. "There is another candidate who has the inside track," he said. "He is a first rate writer for one of the top newspapers in the country, and if I can persuade him to come on board, he has the job."

"But that does not necessarily make him a good public relations man," the woman said. "Does he have the kind of flair and personality that goes into public relations—and understanding of people?"

Somewhat taken aback, the president said, "He's got the right credentials. He can get us into the major media."

It is true that public relations people generally have come from journalistic backgrounds, bringing with them sound ability in communications. Most make the transition successfully from that realm to the college campus. Increasingly, however, people are coming into the field via training in public relations received in college or through experience in corporate, military, and agency public relations. Advertising has yielded some excellent talent for colleges. So, communications background is not a requirement for public relations, particularly not in community colleges.

One of the most successful community college districts in the country had as its director of public relations a woman who had no experience in journalism, none of the traditional qualifications said to be necessary for public relations. But she did have years of experience in the community as a civic leader, understanding and perception of needs and problems, a winning personality, and contacts at all levels of government and with the communications media. She found the necessary technical talent to handle the backup work necessary for the public relation nitty-gritty.

Where to Look

In addition to examining the traditional outlets for public relations personnel, administrators recruiting talent should look at older people in the community who may be searching for ways to contribute and at the same time earn their own livelihoods. Sometimes such people can be spotted among volunteers in bond campaigns or other endeavors related to the college. If "community" in community college is to mean anything, then recruiters should look to the community for people to help carry out the mission. While these situations are exceptional, they are not so exceptional that they should not be pursued. Public relations talent comes in strange dress, often from unlikely quarters. Every effort should be made to tap all available talent pools. Today, when hiring practices are dictated by federal and state affirmative action requirements, it is essential that all possible avenues be explored.

Barring the exceptional, however, the college will look for that person to direct the public relations program who has knowledge and experience in communications, who has displayed an ability to manage people, who has shown proclivity to be creative, to be an idea person, and who seems to have the kind of personality and spirit that will fit into the mix of the community college.

The usual sources for recruiting the kind of person needed are placement agencies, professional organizations, and advertising in professional journals or educational publications. Keep in mind, too, that traditionally the route to the top in education has been through movement from one institution to another, usually from a smaller college to a bigger one and so on. Community colleges also have something else going for them today. Successful four-year college and university people are beginning to look favorably upon the opportunities provided in the community college and upon the innovative down-to-earth nature of these institutions, which is the appropriate climate for nurturing a healthy public relations program. If the college has not had a well-rounded public relations program, it may not be in a position to look inward, but otherwise, that is an obvious first step in attempting to staff the program—in fact, it is mandatory.

Job Titles and Salary

Despite the egalitarian outlook of the community college, human nature and tradition dictate that job titles are important to individuals and to professional groups. And as long as hierarchies or ladder systems of advancement obtain, then the title that goes with the job is important. There are many euphemisms for public relations itself, but whether a person is called director, assistant to the president, vice-president, or dean, will be important to him or her as the individual attempts to cut through the layers of officialdom necessary to get at the message.

The officer should have a title that reflects management or top-level authority. In many four-year institutions, the position has been given the status of vice-president, which means the officer enjoys cabinet status and which clearly mandates that he take his place among the institution's decision makers. In a few places, the term *dean* has been used. That title, by tradition, suggests a more academic role and therefore may confuse various publics, particularly those in the institution. Often the title *presidential assistant* is used, but that is an anomalous title that may obfuscate even more what the job is really about.

The title *director* will do in most community colleges, depending upon what other key officials are called. The point is, the job itself must be treated as a key position in the administrative ranks and the title must convey its importance. If the college has labeled most of its top officials under the president as vice-presidents, then the public relations chief should carry the same title if he is to have the weight needed to work with the other chief administrators.

Salary, too, must be commensurate with that of other executives. The following situation is hypothetical, but not far from the all-too-frequent perceptions of administrators that a public relations executive does not have, and is not worth, the same status and money enjoyed by other executives:

A screening committee meets with the college president to interview applicants for the position of public information officer at a community college in a large multicollege district. The committee is composed of the district director of public information and the community services and institutional research coordinators for the college.

In outlining the requirements of the job, the president emphasizes that his office staff comprises three major positions—those of the two coordinators on the committee and the public information position to be filled. He emphasizes that these are three coequal jobs, that he will rely on and expect the same level of work and effectiveness from all three. He reviews the college's need for public information and says it is at least as important as the need for community services and institutional research.

The district director of public information does not mention it, but he is curious about the fact that the salary for the public information officer position is about 60 percent that for each of the other two positions.

The Job Description

Title: Vice President for Community Relations

General Description: The position will carry responsibility for supporting and implementing the mission and policies of the community college through communications that will generate appropriate public understanding and perceptions of the institution to the end that the college will operate in a healthy supportive climate.

Specific Responsibilities:

1. Sit with the president's council to give advice and input into policies that will have impact on public attitudes
2. Use various techniques and devices in communications to report and interpret college policies, programs, and activities
3. Create and maintain an appropriate program of internal public relations among members of the immediate college family—students, faculty, administrators, trustees
4. Provide advice and assistance to other departments of the institution on matters that may impact on relations with various publics; should be involved in advisory councils and committees set up by some departments
5. Coordinate activities related to fund raising among both private and public sectors
6. Plan a program of alumni relations and carry it out

Though each of these six broad but specific areas of responsibility given in the job description could be broken down into even smaller tasks, if the person chosen is a fully experienced and capable practitioner (and we assume that would be the case), then these guidelines should provide all the direction needed. Many community colleges, it should be acknowledged, treat public relations and development as completely separate functions. Such bifurcation is questionable and should be reexamined where operative.

THE SUPPORT STAFF

The vice-president or director will need some technical assistance. The assumption is that the plan devised for public relations will provide enough budgetary latitude for

the chief executive to staff appropriately for execution of
the tasks assigned to his office. Naturally, some lid has to
be put on the operation to avoid proliferation of jobs and
the rise of tasks to meet personnel available to carry them
out.

It is difficult to single out a typical institution in a
typical setting. The college that is located in the back-
woods, in a rural area, obviously is going to have different
needs, problems—and opportunities—than the college
located in the heart of the big city. Even so, there will be
certain tasks that are common to both, so, in staffing and
organizing an office of public relations, it is appropriate to
look at those jobs that have to be done and then staff from
there.

Since a primary part of the vice-president's time and
energy will be consumed in policy-level work both with
other chief officers and with planning and management of
the public relations program, then it follows that where he
or she will need technical assistance most is in those areas
that are also time consuming and energy burning. In most
institutions, the two areas of public relations that demand
the largest share of attention are (1) public information,
which can embrace press relations, publications, and special
events, and (2) fund raising, which may also cover alumni
relations, resource development at state and national government levels (as well as local campaigns), and development in the corporate and foundation worlds. This
approach can be charted in a simple organizational frame-
work. An example of the way it might look is shown on the
following page.

Keep in mind that these assistants deal with support
activities. Though the director of public information will
maintain day-to-day contact with the press, for example,
the vice-president of public relations will also have close

Vice-President for College Relations

Institutional policy making and intrepretation
Overall planning and development
Department management

Director of Public Information	Director of Development
Press relations	Fund raising:
Special events	Government relations (state,
Publications	national, local)
Speech writing and coordina-	Corporate and foundation
tion of speakers' bureau	relations
	Alumni affairs

---

contact with the media. He or she will be the spokesman for the college, when the president or other executive is not available or may not be required to answer, on questions of policy and perhaps controversial matters. Similarly, the vice-president of public relations will be heavily engaged in planning and directing strategy in fund raising; he or she will in most cases make the first important contact with a major foundation or corporation. The development director will work on strategy, write proposals, and do the necessary leg work that will lead to success in this vital area. All three functionaries will engage in continuous planning, looking constantly at goals and objectives that relate to the total mission of the institution. At the same time, all three will relate closely to all other elements of the college; no program of public relations can be effective if those responsible tend to work in a vacuum, setting themselves off from the mainstream of college life.

The two supportive jobs require certain qualifications. Obviously, the public information officer needs to have a thorough grasp of communications techniques—writing, editing, graphics—particularly if the vice-president is one of these exceptional people who may not have the skills but has the overall leadership ability to run a good public relations program. The public information officer must know the media; must understand the problems of dead-lines, the things that particularly interest editors and broad-cast managers; must have at least a feeling for, if not full grasp of, how to package a message in a publication, report, or other kind of published document.

Likewise, the development officer must have a thorough understanding of the corporate and foundation world; have or develop contacts in state, local, and national govern-ments; and have ability and skill to put together proposals. The best ideas ever invented will fail if they are not properly explained, outlined, packaged if you will, for the consumer. Sad but true. The development officer will often as not have fairly broad experience in public relations, bring-ing to the job an understanding of all aspects of the profession.

Ideally, the two officers will have backgrounds that are somewhat similar with skills and know-how that can be interchangeable. By all means, they must be able to work together. Not only are they supportive of the institutional goals, but they are supportive of each other. Education? Again, these professionals will probably have at least a bachelor's degree. They may have been trained in a school or department of journalism; they may have had a com-bination of education and work experience in communica-tions. Government background may be particularly helpful to the development officer.

MULTICAMPUS OPERATIONS

With many community colleges, small and large, install-ing second, third, and even fourth campus or satellite centers, there arises a serious question of how to cover these bases for public relations. Certainly, what goes on at any of these campuses is just as important as what is taking place at the central campus. In fact, one or more of the satellites, because of location, people being served, program emphasis, or some other factor, may tend to provide more opportunities and possibilities for public relations than the central campus.

Many community college presidents frankly admit that they have not figured out a way to handle the problem. Ideally, they would like to put a full-time specialist on each campus, but that is difficult to sell and perhaps too much to fit into tightly planned budgets. At the very least, however, effort should be made to arrange for someone on each campus, perhaps an English teacher or community service specialist, to serve as the eyes and ears of the public relations department. The person should be asked to carry a reduced teaching load, perhaps giving half time to that assignment and half time to public relations. Under such an arrangement, that person could be expected to:

- call attention of the public relations office to innovations in teaching, unusual people on campus, special events that might serve as the basis for public information, publications, speeches, and the like
- in the case of a person with appropriate skills, rough out reports and press releases that would then be entered into the schedule of public relations material to be issued by the central office.

As the campuses grow larger and the problems become more complex, it will eventually be necessary to create a full-time office staffed by a person or persons qualified in

important areas of public relations. Some campuses already
have gone this route and would now find it difficult to
turn back the clock.

Whatever the arrangements made on the separate campuses, it does not relieve the chief public relations staff of
the responsibility and opportunity to spend considerable
time on each campus. It is important that all the staff
know each of the centers, have good contacts with them,
visit them frequently, and develop proper rapport with
officials on those campuses. Moreover, the staff will find it
refreshing to leave the sanctity of the central campus to go
out where the action is.

EVALUATION

It was once axiomatic that public relations could be
judged and evaluated on the number of mentions in
newspapers or other media. A thick press-clippings book
was enough to justify the existence of the office at the end
of a year. It became recognized, however, that mentions do
not tell the story. In fact, there can even be overcoverage.
People may tire of hearing or reading or seeing articles
about the college, particularly those that convey no real
sense of the mission of the institution.

More important than volume of clippings is what happens as a result. Are publics demonstrating support? Are
people that should be reached taking advantage of the
institution? Are appeals for financial support meeting with
success? What's happening as a result of public relations
with regard to how people think of and act toward the
institution? There are scoffers who will say that if the
college has a good program of education, then that will
suffice. They will credit success with the quality of the
program, rather than with any public relations activity. But

that is a perennial problem that will not go away, and as long as administration feels the need for good public relations, it will not be a serious problem.

Regardless of outside attitudes the public relations office will be constantly evaluating its program through personal contact with its publics, through occasional public opinion surveys, and through tangible results of programs. Some simple evaluative questions that can be used as guidelines are these:

1. Are press releases being used? In their entirety? Completely rewritten? Shortened?
2. Do people refer to publications of the institution when they contact college people? Can attendance or registration be traced, at least in part, to the publications program?
3. Does the official annual report get editorial attention in the newspapers and other media? What kind of letters come to the college as a result?
4. What kind of attendance is there at alumni events? Do alumni respond to fund appeals? Do they show up in assisting with bond campaigns? Can they be counted?
5. In fund raising, the number of dollars obtained is probably evaluation enough, but there are other questions that can be asked. Why did a proposal appeal to one corporation and not to another? Why did the neighboring college receive two million dollars from a government program, while ours only received half a million dollars?

Public relations, no matter how mysterious it may be, is also accountable. Some means of evaluation must be used or there will come a time when the scoffers may win out.

Following is a sample of a simple questionnaire used with fair success by Montgomery College in Maryland to determine how students were attracted to the institution.

QUESTIONNAIRE FOR FALL SEMESTER

We need your help to find out what, where and how students are learning about Montgomery College. Please complete this form.

1. Age: 2. Sex: 3. Residents:

   0 ☐ 16-19   0 ☐ Male   0 ☐ Montgomery County
   1 ☐ 20-24   1 ☐ Female   1 ☐ Maryland (not
   2 ☐ 25 and over   Montgomery)
                                         2 ☐ Out of state

4. Name of high school (only if in Montgomery County) from which you graduated:

   _____

5. Check one

   0 ☐ Enrolling for the first time at any college
   1 ☐ Have attended MC before
   2 ☐ Have attended another college but not MC

6. Check one

   0 ☐ Enrolling in a degree program
   1 ☐ Enrolling as a special student
   2 ☐ Enrolling in early placement program

7. From which of the following did you get information about Montgomery College? (check all that are appropriate)

   0 ☐ Information sent to your   3 ☐ High school counselors
        home   4 ☐ High school teachers
   1 ☐ Newspaper articles   5 ☐ Publications distributed at
   2 ☐ Radio announcements   your school

8. Who influenced you most to enroll at MC? (*check not more than three*)

0 ☐ High school teacher
1 ☐ High school guidance counselor
2 ☐ Parents
3 ☐ College counselor
4 ☐ Student at MC
5 ☐ Former MC students or graduates
6 ☐ High school classmates
7 ☐ Employer

9. Which of the following influenced you most to come to MC? (*check not more than three*)

0 ☐ Location close to home
1 ☐ Location near nation's capital
2 ☐ Course offerings
3 ☐ Athletic program
4 ☐ Cost
5 ☐ Quality of teachers
6 ☐ Overall reputation of the college
7 ☐ Appearance of campus

10. Check the 3 ways you believe people can best be informed about MC.

0 ☐ Displays and exhibits
1 ☐ Information sent to homes
2 ☐ Daily newspaper ads
3 ☐ Weekly newspaper ads
4 ☐ Movies or slide presentations
5 ☐ High school newspaper ad
6 ☐ Newspaper articles
7 ☐ Posters
8 ☐ Radio announcements
9 ☐ Speakers

11. For which 3 things is MC best known?

0 ☐ Art exhibits
1 ☐ Athletic teams
2 ☐ Musical programs
3 ☐ Plays
4 ☐ High academic standards
5 ☐ Courses offered
6 ☐ Quality faculty
7 ☐ Community programs
8 ☐ Satisfied former students

12. How much have you heard on radio about MC? (*check one*)

0 ☐ A great deal
1 ☐ Some
2 ☐ Very little
3 ☐ None

13. How much have you read in newspapers about MC? (*check one*)

0 ☐ A great deal   2 ☐ Very little
1 ☐ Some   3 ☐ None

14. On the following scale put an X in the box at the relative position *you believe* best describes Montgomery College.

    0   1   2   3   4   5   6   7   8

Fair   Good   Excellent   Outstanding

15. On the following scale put an X in the box at the relative position you believe best describes *what other people think* about Montgomery College.

    0   1   2   3   4   5   6   7   8

Fair   Good   Excellent   Outstanding

16. List: 17. List:

The newspapers you *read*   The radio stations you *lis-*
regularly: *ten to most often:*

_____   _____
_____   _____
_____   _____
_____   _____

— THANK YOU FOR YOUR HELP —

Another view of evaluation is provided by John H. Krafft, college relations director at Delta College in Michigan. Essentially, he says that evaluation can be achieved by the development of sound objectives for the program. The degree to which the objectives are met provides some measurement of public relations effectiveness. Mr. Krafft offers some other interesting observations on evaluation:

> I had also written a laboriously churning missive on trying to identify other performance measures, such as (A) The Survey, (B) The In-Depth Interview, (C) The Dollar Indicator, (D) Making of a Millage, (E) Funny Figures, (F) Media Content Analysis, (G) The Publications Syndrome. All of these methods were, more or less, thought to be measureable indicators of PR success by yours truly at one time or another. For example, I decided that a survey of present students asking them where they heard about the college—word-of-mouth, direct mail, radio, television, etc.—would be a persuasive performance measure for various Madison-Avenue-type recruitment efforts. No way. This is murky turf. My suspicion is that all of the impacts, media and personal, on a particular individual probably create an admissions motivation which may or may not turn into the real thing. Then I decided that maybe the dollar indicator was a measure of effectiveness of our alumni program, which neatly avoids all that good will PR. Does the making of a millage suggest true citizenry support? Are 200,000 lives, touched annually by various programs and services, sufficient to suggest that the means, by which these programs and services are brought to the attention of the people for whom they are intended, are effective? Is all my good/bad ink earning district support? Does our wild graphic illustrator offend with his mezzotints? I refer you back to the objectives and their measures as more-modestly stated public relations intentions for which measures of performance can be developed.

Guidelines for Chapter 4 _____

In this chapter, staffing and organizing for public relations have been discussed. It is a difficult subject to generalize because needs depend upon so many variables such as size of institution, its location, and special problems that may exist, but it is obvious that communications must take place whether or not there is an office or a staff. The best job of communications will only be accomplished where there is some expertise, understanding, aggressive direction, and creative thinking. Here are some guidelines:

1. Administrators and trustees must give public relations functions, objectives, and staff appropriate status and support.
2. Planners must act on the premise that a good public relations program will pay for itself and much more, too.
3. Public relations counsel may be called in to set up a new program or modify an existing activity.
4. While the president's office may work out a broad program, it is more appropriate to have a chief executive of public relations on board before specific goals and objectives are set forth.
5. In a model situation, the staff may include a director of public information and a director of development, operating closely with the vice-president.

6. In a multicampus operation, there should be persons assigned, at least on a part-time basis, to public relations.
7. There must be continuous planning and evaluation of the public relations program.
8. Colleges should look to local communities in their recruitment efforts for that exceptional person who may bring community understanding and contacts to bear on the program.
9. The public relations vice-president should be a leader among his or her contemporaries in the administrative hierarchy.

A Family Process _____ 5

"This institution is made up of people," the president said in his annual report, "and it will succeed or fail on how it impacts on their lives and the quality of life in this community.

"The College is not merely a group of buildings, a cluster of classrooms, an array of parking lots, a complex of computers. It is students, young and old, it is their parents, their other relatives, their friends. It is teachers and other staff who want this place to be something. It is the members of our board, the people on advisory committees, who give of their time and energy to help insure that the educational mission is properly carried out.

"This is the people's college."

Too often, in a computerized society, there is a tendency to lose sight of the fact that a college is a thing of people, not of facilities. In the constant struggle to create more classrooms, add new equipment, and build additional structures, the real purpose of the educational institution is overlooked. People come and go, teachers report in and report out, meetings are held and adjourned, progress is heralded in terms of new resources that may be uncovered. The real mission of the institution may be forgotten and obscured by the constant accretion of the tools and materials to carry it out.

The truly effective public relations operation will have as one of its objectives that of reminding, of serving as a kind of conscience for the college, making certain that the human side is constantly communicated. In order to serve as a conscience and to effectively generate interest and support in the institution, the public relations officer must be in and of the people—not set aside in some isolation booth—always open, close to the other members of the college family. One can say, in fact, that the public relations office and staff could not do its job well without being in touch with all other elements of the college, as well as the community. There are two good reasons for making such a statement:

- The public relations office must have a feeling for and be sensitive to attitudes and concerns of others involved in the educational process or it cannot possibly interpret to outsiders the kind of institution being represented. Knowing policies and understanding high-level planning is, as we have indicated, essential; but just as essential is knowing grass roots opinions and feelings about the college.
- Returning for a moment to the parts of the college public relations program, remember that they are many and varied. The point has been established that no community college could reasonably expect to have staff to fulfill all the functions described in that section. To cover all the bases, therefore, will depend upon a high degree of cooperation from all other members of the college family. The public information officer, for example, can be expected to do that headline-getting article on an unusual student, a dedicated faculty member, but he might never have had the opportunity without the cooperation, alertness, and helpfulness of an employee in admissions or a counselor or another faculty member. Or, the development officer may find it

extremely difficult to put together a solid proposal for a government agency for a new curriculum without solid information from a phalanx of educators who understand the problem and are willing to give time and energy to gathering and documenting the need.

W. Emerson Reck, dean of educational public relationists and author of one of the first books in the field, maintains that the public relations office will find the going difficult in the external world if it does not first take into account the needs, concerns, interests, and feeling of the internal publics—often referred to as the family. He enunciated ten principles of public relations in 1946. Here's one that he stressed:

Public relations is a way of life for an entire institution—not the job for a single individual. Although it is sometimes difficult for faculty members, secretaries and students to appreciate the fact, they are among the most important arms of the public relations department. Quite a few institutions, especially smaller ones, emphasize in their literature that a friendly atmosphere prevails on their campuses. Visits to these campuses do not always bear out the truth of these statements, however, because the registrar, a faculty member, a student or possibly a secretary fails to display the friendly spirit which has been advertised as special.[*]

Times were different in 1946. Some horrendous events have occurred in society and on campuses since then. Situations that would not have been tolerated then are accepted as commonplace now. Faculty members do speak out on controversial issues today, both individually and

[*]W. Emerson Reck, *Public Relations: A Program for Colleges and Universities,* (New York: Harper & Row, 1946), p. 11.

collectively; students are no longer puppets to be trotted out on special occasions to show that a warm, friendly, and productive atmosphere obtains on the campus. Although the changes make life more difficult for administrators and certainly for public relations people, most thinkers would agree that the atmosphere is more open, more free, much healthier today.

For good or bad, faculty and students continue to be the chief public relations emissaries of the institution. They live and work in the community, they carry whatever impressions or perceptions they have of it, good, bad, or indifferent, to other people. The people on the campus, not the buildings and computers, are the grist for the public relations mill. What they say about the institution in their individual conversations, or in their public activities, constitute public relations. What they do on campus, how they perform, and who they are provide the ingredients for showing and demonstrating how effective the institution may be in its program.

WORKING ON FAMILY ATTITUDES

Public relations men and women cannot dictate attitudes, nor should they. There are no puppets on college campuses today, particularly not on the community college campus. Nonetheless, the college, in part through its public relations office, must seek to bring about understanding of the institution among its immediate family before it can hope to persuade other publics that the college is an exciting, vital resource. It is no mean task. The great mixture of students—some of them old, some of them young, some of them poor, some of them middle class— would seem to defy any concerted effort to inculcate any kind of general good spirit about their institution. Coming and going at all hours, they are even difficult to reach in a physical sense.

Perhaps that is one of the reasons why most community colleges throw up their hands in disgust when the term *alumni relations* is used. "How can you expect loyalty when these people are so fleeting?" is a comment often heard, or "They are eventually going to get their baccalaureate degrees somewhere else, so why expect them to remember this college?" and "People who are going out to take jobs after two years won't be able to contribute much to the college anyway." Thus, there is little effort from the start of the student's campus life to breed into him any feeling for the institution or to involve him in the total structure of the institution so that he will feel something more than that he is just going to classes and working.

Let me cite a small but perhaps significant example. The parents of a young man who entered a community college were delighted at the end of his first year to learn that he had made the dean's list. They had had doubts about his going to the college and about his ability to hold down a part-time job and still come out at the top. He had not been a good student in high school; he was not academically inclined.

Nothing could really have dampened their delight— except that the computer printout announcing that the boy was on the dean's list left something to be desired. Surely, the college could have provided at least a form note from the dean's office rather than a barely readable printout—not calculated to instill any good feeling about the institution.

Another example worth repeating concerns a young foreigner, whose mother worked for a Washington, D.C. embassy so he was able to join her there at midyear. Both wanted him to enter a suburban community college. They found, however, that although he was on the scene in time

to enter for the second semester, the English-equivalency
test required for entry had already been administered by
the college and would not be given again until later in the
year. He had all the other prerequisites for entry. The
student and his mother found that the test could be taken
elsewhere and asked the college for permission to do so.
The college turned him down.

It could be argued that there is no reason for a local
community college be concerned with some foreigner. After
all, its first obligation is to the local taxpaying public. But
in this instance, even if that were a justifiable attitude, the
college was serving a Washington suburb in which many of
its clients are sons and daughters of nationals of other
countries—people who live in and support the community
through home owning or leasing and purchasing of goods.
Moreover, many of them are in the community to stay, to
live forever, eventually to become citizens.

What happened in this situation had several ill effects.
It left a bad taste, not only about the college, but about
the community and about a country. True, colleges must
have efficient procedures, must operate by rules, must not
constantly make exceptions, but in the community college,
we talk about the open door, concern with the individual,
the people's college. There must be some flexibility, some
willingness to give if these expressions are to mean anything
at all.

What do these examples mean for family public relations? They mean that the public relations office ought to
be generating and insisting on public relations consciousness
among other members of the family. In the case of the
dean's list, the public relations office might offer a simple
but helpful suggestion that congratulatory letters from the
president or dean be sent to those who make it. Such
letters could be a simple but effective tool for generating a

better attitude toward the institution. The case of the foreign student's English-equivalency test is perhaps more difficult. It was undoubtedly considered a routine matter and it probably never went—at least in the college—beyond the admission's clerk's desk. But public relations staff should make it their business to know how such problems are handled, and to offer, not inflict, helpful advice to those responsible.

On young and old alike, how they are handled at the admissions point, in the mix of registration, or in contacts with the bureaucracy, unfortunately, creates lasting impressions. It is essential that these areas be of concern to the public relations staff. I do not suggest that the public relations staff become spies or try to take responsibility for all the rules, regulations, processing, and handling of people. But they ought to know the procedures of the institution; they ought to be aware of obstacles; they ought to be cognizant of pressure points that arise. More important, they ought to take it upon themselves to do their best to insure that the small crises are kept to a minimum, if not avoided altogether. Staff in other departments which have daily contact with people may not even be aware of practices that dismay and confuse people. Their job descriptions usually will not spell out a public relations function. So subtly, or subliminally, some office must take responsibility for inculcating proper attitudes, and certainly some empathy, with the problems of those entering the college so that perceptions will be improved, not impaired.

There are several approaches to alleviating the problems created by poor public relations at the front desk, as it were. The chief public relations officer, of course, should get the message across to deans and heads of departments at staff meetings. It would not be out of line for the public relations office to contrive to place questions of internal public relations on the agenda for at least one staff meeting per year. Ways to improve the image at points of people contact might well be the subject for such a meeting. Then, department heads would be expected to brief their own staffs on better ways to relate to incoming students or other persons who have contact with the institution. Some points that ought to be made:

1. Are telephone calls taken in a courteous, cheerful, and helpful manner?
2. Can some red tape, such as that which frequently occurs in registration lines, be eliminated or at least reduced to a minimum? How can computerized registration be made more human?
3. Do all staff know generally what the college offers, what its program is, so that they can answer such questions intelligently?
4. Do they know the college's facilities, where certain departments are located, where various departments are housed?
5. Are they willing to take an extra step, go a little out of the way to make visitors and/or first-time students feel a bit more comfortable in the rarified college atmosphere?
6. Do they feel any sense of pride, of belonging to a worthwhile place or thing, as employees of the college?
7. Are they encouraged to come up with problem-solving ideas and new approaches to the work that will bring about efficiencies, as is so common in industry?
8. Does the college have any mechanisms for rewarding people, for giving them recognition for doing unusual or outstanding work?

9. Are top officials acquainted with, or do they take the trouble to become acquainted with, personnel who may be doing the so-called drudgery of the institution?
10. Is opportunity provided for discussion of the college's purposes and goals at levels below the top of the hierarchy?

Discussions of these questions may lead to answers that will result in more positive public relations attitudes on this vital front. These questions and others may serve as a guide for developing a handbook on the institution which could be placed in the hands of every employee. Efforts to bring about better approaches to the jobs of classified personnel can also be made through employee newsletters, through meetings, and through memoranda from the president and other officials.

PUBLIC RELATIONS AND STUDENTS

Too often, students are not even aware of the existence of the public relations office. Yet, ironically, they are the product, the living demonstrations, of whether the institution is carrying out the mission, whether it is doing the kind of job that other publics can support enthusiastically. Conversely, public relations staff all too often fail to involve students in their efforts or to identify with students other than in a professional sense. They see students as grist for good copy, statistics for the annual report on enrollments or the story about matriculation, or creators of a disturbance that makes controversial headlines. Yet these are the people who are going out into the community, into jobs, into churches, into social groups conveying the college message, or more likely, their impressions and perceptions of the institution. We can hope that most of the impressions will be positive and supportive, but there is no program in public relations or any other area that can insure against some negative attitudes, some deepfelt hurts about the institution. But the public relations office is missing an important bet if it does not gamble a little of its time and energy on the student as a part of the family who can help in the campaign to win friends and influence other people.

No one can expect students, especially in this day and age, to engage in hyperbolic praise of the college or to spout public relations puffery. Any attempt to create public relations parrots of students will fall flat on its face. They would see through it. They would become unbelievers rather than believers. But young people do like to be involved. They like to offer their opinions, and they will work if given a chance, so the key word in connection with students is *involvement*. Such involvement may not only result in better attitudes on the part of the students, but may net some good ideas for public relations itself.

Before outlining ways to involve students, we should ask what results we want to have from such involvement. In general, the answer is that we want students to have a sense of belonging to an important, progressive, useful institution that is contributing to their self-fulfillment as well as to the well-being of others. In generating this kind of involvement and bringing about the desired results, the hope is that this is the kind of impression they will convey to others. A desirable byproduct would be that students would also bring fresh new ideas into the public relations program and that occasionally some of them would, or could be put in a position to, take some positive steps to help implement the program.

In what ways can the desired involvement be brought about?

1. Make sure that orientation meetings for new students carry the public relations message. Too often, such meetings overlook institutional mission and goals and dwell only on procedures, how to find the bathrooms, where to inquire about jobs.
2. Place in the hands of the students printed materials that give some of the flavor of the mission and the program of the college.
3. Make certain that as many as possible of the people who work in the institution go out of their way to know students.
4. Arrange for students to work in the public relations office, making them emissaries of that office to the larger group.
5. Establish a public relations advisory committee made up of students. Use this committee to obtain new ideas for public relations. Use it as a sounding board for practices and programs already in existence.
6. Give students roles to play in campaigns, special events, ceremonies, and other programs that bring people to the campus.
7. Be helpful to student groups in publicizing their events and programs, even if the activities are not directly related to the educational mission of the institution. If the college, for example, has given approval for the holding of a rock concert under the sponsorship of a particular group, then the public relations office ought to offer its services on a limited basis to make that program a success.
8. Make students aware of the existence of the public relations office. Make certain that the door is as open to them as it is to other members of the college family.

In working out these and other simple mechanisms for student involvement, the public relations office is not merely dealing with the present, with the impressions and attitudes that will be conveyed at the moment; it is laying the ground work for some kind of alumni work that will take place in the future. If the students do not feel good about the college when they are there, on the campus, then they are not apt to remember it fondly in later years, and if they do not retain some fond memories, then they are not likely to come forward when support and assistance is sought.

Far too many alumni forget the community college when they list their educational backgrounds in directories, registries, and promotional material. Some prominent Americans listed in *Who's Who in America* do not include in their biographical sketches the fact that they graduated from junior or community colleges. Either they don't want to remember or it's just an oversight. In either case, the college has failed to provide the kind of experience that the alumnus is to list.

THE FACULTY AND PUBLIC RELATIONS

The faculty are perhaps more suspicious of public relations than students or any other family group. They tend to think of the function as an adjunct of the president's office, that it is somehow or other suspect, out to get the goods on teachers who may not be following the party line or who may be critical of the administration. This attitude is not improved by public relations officers who tend to put faculty at arm's length and not to notice them unless they (1) achieve some honor that cannot be overlooked or (2) become involved in some controversial matter that must be dealt with from an official point of view.

Some colleges seem to go out of their way to create

conflict situations between faculty and public relations staff. For example, one community college used its public relations officer as the negotiator representing the administration in collective bargaining sessions with faculty. It is true that public relations men must often wear many hats, but it is unthinkable for such an officer at once to represent the institution's public relations and serve in an adversary role between groups. One large body of that institution will never trust him again.

Trust is as vital when dealing with faculty as with any group. These are thinking people who are at once entrusted with the shaping of minds and the carrying out of the real mission of the institution. What they do and say will have profound effect on the feelings and attitudes, not only of students, but of most elements in the larger community. Moreover, many will be directly involved in varied activities outside the campus—church, civic organizations, professional groups, politics. The college's worth may be judged on their worth, their reputations, their actions.

Finally, faculty are second only to students as a source of positive public relations ammunition. How they teach, what past experience they bring to their jobs, their avocations and special interests, their experimentation and research (yes, such does and should occur on community college campuses), and their thoughts and ideas constitute important parts of the recipe for good public relations. For the public relations man dealing with faculty, there are two very basic, intertwined problems related to trust and understanding:

- How do members of the public relations office really get to know the faculty member, what he is all about, the "story" that is in every teacher, what he has to offer to buttress the message? The campus is a big place with many personalities to be dealt with.

- Assuming that the public relations office has found a way to get beyond the faculty member as teacher, to learn about him as a person, how does it gain the trust that, one the one hand, will give it free use of the material gathered and, on the other hand, cause the faculty member to think of the college when he tells his story or makes an appearance that will provide appropriate visibility? In short, how can the college get some benefit to rub off on it from the unusual teacher who receives fame or recognition in his own right? There is the case of the community college teacher who, because of his unusual method of teaching and a witty personality, appeared time after time on a national TV talk show. His identification with the college was minimal, at best, so he gave no indication of what type of college he taught at, why it had him, or what teaching there was like. True, the TV show was interested in the man and his approach to teaching, but maybe, with a little encouragement, that man could have worked in a few telling lines about the institution that employed him and made it possible for his kind of teaching to go on. Certainly, it would have been worth a good PR try.

On the first problem, the public relations office should maintain up-to-date files on all faculty members or have access to files in departments where they work—not files dealing with job performance or personnel records, but biographical files that provide information on past experience and special activities. Such files, of course, save a lot of time and energy for the public relations office when a fairly routine story comes up on a faculty member—his election to an office in a professional organization or her leadership of a study tour to a distant country. More important, constant review of these files will turn up the unusual, the special activity or experience that will show a person of high quality and inventive nature, which can be converted into a major story or become a part of a proposal for a grant to engage in some new research.

In addition to the need for good files, the public relations officer should make it a point to become as well acquainted as possible with all teachers and certainly with all department heads, who can become good sources of information about their staffs and who will tip the public relations office to information that may be useable in the program. One approach is to treat each department as a beat, much the same way a newspaper assigns reporters to various areas of community life. The office then assigns staff to those beats on a regular basis, rather than waiting until something turns up of its own accord.

Such an approach will also give the public relations staff opportunity to get to know faculty members on a personal basis, to hear their gripes and complaints as well as to learn more about their accomplishments and interests. While there are suspicions of public relations, there is at the same time a tendency on the part of others to let their hair down in the presence of public relations people when the setting is informal and personal. Perhaps there is the feeling that the information passed along will get back to the top. At any rate, the newspaper beat approach is effective and can be most enjoyable.

The second problem, that of obtaining the trust and assistance of the faculty member in conveying the institutional message, is obviously more difficult. It is too much to assume that the faculty member will automatically feel a great devotion and loyalty to the college. In fact, for one reason or another, the opposite is often true, but the public relations office can at least make an effort to show interest and project the idea that the teacher can be an emissary of good will for the institution—perhaps by pointing up the teacher's importance to the mission and program of the college.

A public relations counselor, invited to advise a midwestern community college on its public relations program, was astounded to find that faculty had never really been approached on the subject of their role in public relations. This came out after the president obligingly honored a request of the counselor to arrange for a meeting with a representative group of faculty members. The faculty, too, were surprised because their opinions of the institution, its image in the community, its techniques for public relations, had never before been sought. They were, as might be expected, very vocal, but in tune and pleased to be asked to talk about the subject. Out of that one meeting came some very excellent suggestions for public relations. Just as with students, it is not a matter of trying to brainwash intelligent people into mouthing hyperboles or parroting a public relations message; it is simply a matter of saying to these people, "Hey, maybe we have some problems that you can help solve," or, "We seem to be in a rut in our public relations program. Do you have any ideas for us?"

Public relations ought to be the subject of at least one general faculty meeting during the year. Each department should give attention to the subject once or twice a year. The role of the public relations office should be made clear and its interest in serving faculty interests explained and made understandable. Confidence and trust may come as a result. The public relations office should also have a public relations advisory committee made up of faculty—to bounce ideas off, from which to get soundings of misperceptions of the institution and new ideas, and just become better acquainted. As for tying the college message to the individual who may in his or her own right receive important attention for something he or she has done, perhaps the approaches cited above will bring about understanding and interest that will help the faculty member to become more cognizant of this service to be performed. Obviously, you can lead a faculty member to this goal—but you can't make him indulge. But if he is given some sense of how important his special contributions are to the overall good of the institution, then he will be more apt to think of the institution when he makes public appearances, shows up on TV, or is interviewed by some national publication. After all, he must be persuaded that, though his "thing" may be his, it may be more salable, more visible, because he practices it or engages in it in a community college setting, that perhaps he owes something to that institution for providing the backdrop for his fame or fortune outside the confines of the classroom.

Certainly, faculty should be invited to participate in and take responsibility for certain public relations activities. They should be encouraged to take part in TV talk shows, to give of their knowledge on public matters, to be the resident experts on issues and problems in society that are common to all communities. The head of an economics department in a Pennsylvania college did a study on the impact of the college on the community from a financial standpoint, covering such matters as dollars spent by the institution itself, the contribution of salaries toward the economy, taxes paid by employees, and how the college helped to meet manpower needs of the community. Such a study might have gathered dust on a library shelf had not good public relations persisted.

College teachers are usually considered the founts of knowledge and wisdom in any community, and they are generally quite amenable to making their views known. If the public relations officer does not get involved in their act, the story might turn out quite differently than otherwise. Giving faculty public visibility gives the college public visibility, adds to the professional growth of the individual, and contributes to more effective communication, in an atmosphere of trust and confidence, on the part of the communications office.

TRUSTEES AND PUBLIC RELATIONS

Trustees are usually important people in the community. They may be civic leaders and certainly they will be community leaders if they carry out their role as directors of the college, or other postsecondary educational institution, appropriately and responsibly. More than likely, the group will be mixed in terms of professional backgrounds and the kinds of careers they are pursuing in their own working lives. The institution, of course, will probably have little to do with who they are and what they represent or what kind of experiences they bring to the trusteeship, especially if the board is an elected body. So, until they become members of the Board, they will not figure importantly in the plans and programs of the college or of its public relations office. Often, however, those elected to the board are persons who have played an active role in promoting some aspect of college development or have shown more than passing interest in the institution. In some cases, they may also have been critics and have sought trusteeship in order to straighten things out. The latter kind of board member obviously presents special kinds of challenges and creates unusual demands on the public relations office as well as on other elements in the institution.

Whatever the background, whatever they may bring to the board in terms of understanding or feelings for or against the institution, the board member becomes an extremely important element in college public relations. What he or she says publicly or informally may have far-reaching repercussions on attitudes of other people toward the institution. Of course the direct actions taken by the board in developing policies and setting goals have immediate and urgent impact on the public relations program that is to be developed. Board actions, whether popular or unpopular, must be reported and interpreted. Unscheduled, unofficial comments by individual board members may come back to haunt the public relations officer. Some board members may unwittingly make statements about the institution that are inaccurate, a situation which may then have to be unsnarled by the public relations office, carefully treading that thin line between fairness in reporting and causing the board member to appear uninformed or a poor representative.

Moreover, what a board member does in his "real life" may become synonymous with the educational institution with which he is associated. A story is told about a chairman of a college board who was also president of a local bank. It was during a period when times were bad and the bank was foreclosing on many home owners who had defaulted on loans. The bank and the college became intertwined in citizens' minds, and people began to identify the foreclosures with the college rather than with the bank. The college, in short, was taking away their homes. It was an irrational notion, of course, but people become irrational in times of stress. The problem was ameliorated in the end by the resignation of the bank president as chairman of the

college board, but it took many years to repair the damage
that had been done. The college suffered great losses in
support and confidence before its fortunes were eventually
turned around.

So the actions of the board, both unofficially and
officially, both in their capacities as board members and in
their positions in the community, both as a collective unit
and as individuals, have something to do with the public
relations strategies and plans of the institution. They can
do more to elevate an institution than any other single
group; on the other hand, they can rend it asunder through
infighting and dissidence. Whatever the case, their participation presents new dimensions for the public relations
operation. No public relations plan can be developed, much
less executed, without some consideration of its implications relative to the board.

First, let's look at the role of the public relations office
with regard to the official work of the board. How does
the office in its everyday routine relate to the board of
trustees? What does it do for them, how does it coordinate
its activities with the desires and wishes of the board? In
general, the public relations office will provide staff services
for the board through the office of the president and will
reflect board actions and concerns in public reports, proposals, and publications. It will provide input and background for the board on what kind of response will be
forthcoming from the community with regard to proposed
board actions. It will take part, when called for, in
discussions dealing with public opinion or perceptions of
the institution and its programs. It will not become the
personal press agent for the chairman or any individual
member of the board; it will not take sides when the board
becomes divided on a particular issue; it will not provide
special services to any board member with respect to his

professional work away from the college. Here is an outline of the specific role of public relations with regard to the board:

1. Provide information to the press and thus to the community on new board members, appointed or elected, as they take office. Although routine, this kind of dissemination will get attention that is most important to the college cause.
2. See to it that board members receive, on a regular basis, copies of college press releases, publications, newsletters, official speeches of the president, and other material that will keep the board member abreast of and thoroughly informed on the institu- tion's programs. The board member, keep in mind, can give only a small portion of his or her time to college work. Although time-consuming, it is helpful to the busy board member if this informational includes briefing papers in which events and activi- ties reported more fully in the other publications are condensed for easy, quick reading.
3. Assist the president and other administrators in drawing up various reports for board meetings, per- haps putting together summaries of lengthy papers and documents as directed by the president.
4. Assist the president and other administrators in setting an agenda for the board.
5. At most board meetings as a member of the top administrative team, help interpret what may be going on in the institution, report on public opinion, and offer any suggestions that may be called for with regard to the public relations position of the college.
6. Handle representatives of the press who might be present, providing them with background material in

advance of the meeting, assisting them in getting the
record straight following the meeting, and issuing
full reports of the meeting to the press, whether
present or not, within a reasonable time after the
meeting.

7. Where the board is considering a controversial issue
or a matter of great public concern, be prepared, at
the discretion and direction of the chief administrator, to call a press conference. If possible, such
conferences should be held off until the next day so
that the parties have time to put together honest
and accurate statements on the issue. In such cases,
the president of the college will serve as the chief
spokesman, although other board members, perhaps
those with dissenting opinions, should be involved if
they so desire. It is better to have such dissenting
opinions aired at the offical college press conference
rather than at meetings called by the individual
dissenter or dissenters.

8. Encourage and assist board members, particularly the
chairman, to make public speeches on the college's
mission and objectives. Some of the requests that
besiege the president might often to good advantage
be turned over to the chairman of the trustees—if
the chairman is properly informed by public relations on the subject to be discussed.

9. Depending on scheduling and time, the president's
office will encourage individual board members to
write about the meaning of the institution in professional journals and magazines—assist in putting the
material together.

10. Encourage and assist board members in taking
active part in fund campaigns, making use of their
personal and professional contacts. Board members

can often open doors to foundations and corporations that might otherwise be closed.

These are some of the major areas with regard to boards which will occupy the public relations officer's time and energy. The items cited here are essentials for a good public relations program. The creative, thinking public relations staff may come up with many other ways in which members of the board can become active in public relations on a positive basis. Often, board members may have far more regard for and understanding of good public relations than do other elements in the family, because frequently they are involved in it and practice it in their own professional lives. They will usually be responsive, therefore, to what may appear to be demands on their time that will go beyond the call of duty. After all, they are public people or more often than not they would not be serving on boards.

One question that comes up automatically in considering the role of the board with regard to public relations, or the role of public relations offices in dealing with trustees, is that of how closely the board member is involved in college activities. How well is he or she known at the college? How well does he or she, on the other hand, know the college program, the kinds of people it is serving, and the faculty who are directing the learning process? Observation would tend to confirm that board members are on hand for their official meetings and present for ceremonies such as dedications and graduations, but their dealings with and participation in the real life of the institution are often minimal.

The whole premise of this book is that good public relations that enhance and advance the mission of the institution depend on understanding of the job and appreciation of the people and the programs that are used in carrying it out. Therefore, it follows that those who set policies and give guidance and direction to the mission ought also to have the opportunity to become more involved. Time is an essential element here. Involvement cannot be listed as a part of the board assignment, or there probably would be few takers, but many board members would welcome the opportunity to get to know the institution better than they can from the pinnacle of "boarddom." It may not be merely a matter of inviting them to do so, however; some coaxing and encouragement may be required.

There are certain dangers inherent in such a proposal. Rather than involvement, the institution may be encouraging meddling beyond the call of the official board role. Because of this danger, there is a tendency to hold the board at arm's length, honoring and recognizing them at official functions, but making little effort to bring them into the unofficial fold of the family. Those who take this attitude may be overlooking the fact that better understanding usually results in better relations. If a question comes up about a new teaching technique or a new program, the board member who has been exposed to the situation may better represent it in his own dealings with various publics than if he were not aware of it nor involved in any way.

Moreover, how can any board member understand and interpret the kinds of postsecondary education institutions that are contributing to needs of millions of Americans today without at least a brush with students? One way in which board members can be provided with an opportunity to get to know students and faculty better is through seminars and talk sessions in which the board members are the discussion leaders. Such sessions could deal with college programs, but they might also concern themselves with larger issues in society. The board member, because of his or her experience and background, would have something to contribute that would be beneficial to the educational process and at the same time would learn something about teachers, about students, and about the institution.

The role of the public relations office in bringing about board participation and involvement is catalytic. Where there is a sense that board involvement is not taking place, it may be up to that office to make that clear to other members of the official family and then simply to raise the questions, Why not more involvement? and How can such be programmed? Obviously, what form involvement should take will be up to the president and other members of the administrative team. Some chief administrators as well as some public relations officers may feel that this kind of effort is beyond the call, but I am dealing here with the total public relations effort at its best, which calls for staffing and programming that will require imagination and willingness to gamble on programs in which there may be some risks, but where the opportunities outweigh those dangers. The public relations staff that does not have that willingness, that imagination, will have only a routine operation concerned with problems rather than opportunities.

Postsecondary education of all kinds has been in a crisis position for the last several years. It is not likely that the situation will change in the foreseeable future. Just as the learning leaders must be creative while becoming more accountable, so should the molders and leaders of public opinion be open to new approaches to the job. Those who are truly creative will go far beyond what has been outlined here.

Guidelines for Chapter 5 _____

In this chapter, other groups within the college community—the immediate family who are vital to the public relations program—have been discussed. The public relations office will of necessity relate closely to these members of the college family and will find among them the best tools for generating and maintaining solid support for the institution. Here are some guidelines:

1. An institution of postsecondary education is made up of people—its lifeblood. The college public relations program must take into account and take advantage of the opportunities provided by the institution's people.
2. Too often, people are obscured by facilities, new machines, and building programs. Such things are vital, of course, but they must be put to work for people.
3. Public relations should constantly be aware of the fact that faculty and students are the chief emissaries of the institutions. What they say and do will have major impact on the public relations stance of the institution.
4. Routine activities of the institution, such as those that take place in admissions offices, often have tremendous impact on the attitudes of people

toward the institution. They should be monitored from a public relations standpoint for ways in which they can be improved and serve the public relations job better.

5. Classified staff should be given an opportunity to understand their role in public relations; an interest in and appreciation of the institution should be inculcated so that this will rub off on those with whom they come in contact.

6. Faculty may tend to be suspicious of public relations activities. This tendency must be overcome, and if at all possible, turned around so that faculty will turn on for the institution.

7. Students and faculty can take active roles in certain kinds of public relations programs, particularly those that require volunteer workers and insight from these segments of the family.

8. Faculty and students can serve as sounding boards for public relations programs and policies. Programs that may appear on the surface to be working well might turn out to be extremely negative in the eyes of these publics.

9. Students and faculty members, if given the chance, may have some good and workable ideas that ought to be tapped by public relations. Public relations is not a field that is narrow and confining; it ought to be open to fresh approaches and recommendations.

10. Boards of trustees, advisors, directors, have an official role to play in public relations. Their words and policies may be an index to what the various publics think of the institution. How their actions and pronouncements are conveyed and interpreted to the public is of vital importance.

11. Services of the public relations office with regard to the board are many and varied; they should be fully clarified, understood, and approved by the chief executive officer.

12. Based on the premise that better understanding leads to better public relations on all fronts, the board of directors ought to be encouraged to become involved in college life, to get to know students, faculty, and others central to the learning process. The public relations office has a role to play in encouraging such participation and in seeing that avenues are cleared for interaction. However, such involvement must be well coordinated and have the full support and participation of the chief executive.

Following the central points cited in this chapter, the public relations office, having dealt positively with the opportunities provided by the people in the institution, can better deal with the other publics, or, put the other way around, since it will already be dealing with those publics, in no way can it afford to ignore or bypass the family, for their treatment, their involvement, their participation in the program will have much bearing on the care and feeding of the other publics outside the institution.

The Other Publics _____ 6

"This is an open door institution," the first line of the typical promotional brochure noted. "This school is set up to provide something for everybody. It is many things to many people."

"This institution operates at low cost to students; its admissions policies are flexible; it maintains many programs for adults as well as young people."

"This is democracy's college, in and of the community, serving all needs, all interests, prepared to respond to requests of the many as well as the few," the brochure goes on. "This is the people's college."

The above quotes reflect the information contained in the typical college catalog, its annual report, or the many promotional brochures, speeches, and other documents that will be the responsibility of the public relations office. There is growing evidence that what such brochures say is not mere hyperbole, not simply public relations fantasy. Community colleges *are* touching on most lives in the typical community—and having deep and direct impact on many.

What does this mean for public relations? Traditionally, most colleges plan their public relations programs around specific publics. Many of the older, four-year institutions could delineate with ease the publics they were trying to reach, simply by the process of elimination. While they might want the blue collar community on their side, for example, they probably would not list this public high in the order of priorities, for obvious reasons. Sons and daughters of blue collar workers would not typically be going to college, and blue collar workers would not be expected to contribute financially to the institution, except by the taxes they pay which might eventually be put toward the institution.

The community college, or the vocational school, however, has declared its commitment to all the people, to all strata of society. Its publics are the general public—everybody. So why think in terms of specific groups? Perhaps the best answer to that is that the institutional message must be couched in different language and disseminated in different ways for different groups. For example, the professional segment of the community might not be turned on by emphasis on the technical programs of the institution, but the labor segment would. Or, the public relations challenge might be to find ways to promote the technical side of the institution's program among professional people by emphasizing how development of appropriate support personnel would alleviate many of their manpower problems. The labor segment, on the other hand, might be given the hope not only of better jobs, but that those who can benefit will be prepared for bigger and better things at the professional level.

Looking at the "publics" stratagem from these standpoints, it is just as important, if not more so, to try and identify specific publics of the community college, even though its purpose is to serve everyone. A list of these publics should add up to the whole community. Certainly, there will be times when the message or an issue should be made loud and clear to everybody as the college reaches out for total support, but on some smaller issues or in advancing a particular curriculum or program, it will be more appropriate to concentrate on a specific audience. Not only will such a flexible approach be more effective in terms of the public relations objective, it will also result in budgetary savings and savings in staff time and energy. These obviously are important considerations for the institution as its public relations staff face up to the myriad responsibilities that must be carried out.

EXTERNAL PUBLICS IN THE BROAD SENSE

For planning purposes and to make the job easier to harness, the public relations office can think of external publics as those not involved directly and on a day-to-day basis in the operations of the institution, as contrasted with the internal publics—students, faculty, administrators, trustees, and classified personnel. However, some of the persons and groups external to the institution have more contact with it than others. The externality is a matter of degree, and that raises a rather interesting question of whether it's easier to deal with and through those who know little or have less contact than those who are intimately involved.

Be that as it may, the institution depends on outsiders to make decisions, to cast the votes, and to proffer support—that will make the advancement program click. Just as a politician must look at his potential support in terms of broad segments of the public, so must the postsecondary educational institution. There is one basic difference, however, in this analogy; that is, the politician may simply write off a particular segment as impossible to penetrate—as a group that cannot possibly be put in his or her column—then concentrate on those segments that are more likely to provide enough votes to secure the election.

A community-centered institution of postsecondary education cannot legitimately write off any segment. In fact, it has to do the contrary. It must be far more aggressive, much more concerned, with that segment of the public which seems to be against policies and programs of the college or school. It must do so without neglecting other segments, lest these groups become alienated as well. Historically, community colleges, if not many of the other two-year units of postsecondary education, grew out of general public concern for meeting new needs and filling educational gaps. In such cases, most segments will give at least token support to the institution. Good public relations can turn token into active support.

What are these broad segments of the public that constitute the external audiences? Certainly, as previously indicated, the professional people of the community are vital. Counted among these are doctors, lawyers, and educators. They are important because they tend to be opinion leaders whose views and comments are courted by the media, they command important resources, and they are often in positions of political leadership. In general, this segment of the public will not have a personal interest or relationship in community colleges, technical institutes, or vocational schools. They will not have had any exposure to the kind of education offered by such institutions, and they will not steer their own sons and daughters toward them (although that is becoming less true). This group will tend to have do-gooding attitudes and see the broader picture and the need for expanding educational opportunity in society.

Labor was also mentioned earlier on. Certainly no group has gained more from the advent of accessible postsecondary institutions of higher education than the workers of the society. Until the doors were opened more widely and the "new" institutions began to make an impact, the current generation of American laborers came up without college experience of any kind. Finally there was hope for upward mobility for their own sons and daughters and even for the parents, who could go back to school for better jobs, advancement, or fun. This group can be counted in the win column but must be courted and contacted along with the other external publics.

The business community is another positive supporter. No other group experiences more immediately the results of the college or school's work, for they employ, either part time or full time, the products of the institution. They benefit directly from the work of the institution. The college represents a source of labor that may even determine whether a corporation places an installation in a particular community. More and more companies, before expanding to a particular area, ask the question, Is there a community college or technical institute in the area? The president of one large company reported that a team from the company not only investigated whether a community college existed, but made preliminary arrangements with that institution to provide training programs for personnel of the proposed plant. Small businesses are attracted to the notion that they can obtain better-trained personnel. Moreover, the business community looks at the college as a large employer and a business that plows resources into the economy. Its employees have purchasing power; the institution must buy equipment and supplies and build new buildings, all of which supports the local economy.

Ethnic groups have become increasingly more important to missions and objectives of all institutions of postsecondary education. While such groups may contain persons from the business community, from labor, and from the professions, there will be many occasions when a

particular ethnic group will become a segment all its own,
united on a particular issue or problem. When that problem
has to do with the college or technical school, then it
becomes necessary for the institution, through its public
relations staff, to deal with this public directly. In its daily
routine, the public relations office will constantly be cognizant of and concerned with attitudes and opinions of the
ethnic groups, either collectively, or broken down into
smaller subgroups. The outlook of the Chicano community
on a particular issue may be far different from that of the
black community. Strategies may be different for each
group. There is a good deal of backslapping about what
many postsecondary educational institutions have done for
minorities, but the fight remains uphill. Some blacks,
Chicanos, and American Indians believe that their interests
are being given little more than token attention.

What does the fact that there are large segments of the
public, large and significant external audiences, to be
reached mean for the public relations staff? It means
homework and special attention to the use of the tools of
the public relations profession, and it calls mainly for
sensitivity to the concerns and interests of these broad
segments. Some specific activities can be listed:

1. The public relations office should make an effort to
   know what these segments are thinking about and
   what they are concerned about. This can be done
   through personal contact with leadership and
   through careful study of newspaper reports and
   editorials reflecting views of various segments. For
   example, if labor appears to be complaining that
   industry is not responsive to training or educational
   needs of workers, then there may be implications for
   the college—immediate or in the future.

2. The public relations office needs to be certain that members of these broad segments are represented on college advisory committees, included on the platforms at major college events, and invited to address student and other college groups.
3. Some publications—reports and brochures—should be aimed directly at particular groups. Mailing lists should be compiled and used when opportunity presents itself.
4. Most of the major groups have media within their own ranks. Releases and articles that would have special appeal to the groups should be directed to such media.
5. The public relations office should work to develop sensitivity to nuances and terminology that may reflect on minorities particularly, and apply it to the treatment of all copy, whether aimed at specific minority groups or at the total institution audience.

SPECIFIC AUDIENCES

While the overall public relations program will constantly be alert to sensitivities of broad segments of the public, the staff will be dealing much of the time with specific audiences or publics that can make direct contributions to the progress of the institution. Success in working with and through the specific publics will have much to do with how successful the institution is in obtaining the support of the general community.

The media, of course, constitute an audience in themselves. While in theory, broadcasters, newspapers, and magazines reflect general attitudes, concerns, and criticisms, they are still people, a small but powerful group who do not always reflect what they believe the community may want or need. They are human, in short, and the public relations officer will be dealing with them as individuals. The public relations officer is the person from the college who comes in most frequent contact with the media. If they do not respect him or her, they may not respect the college. The way to gain such respect is to be fair, honest, and understanding of deadlines, writing styles, and the like. While creating a climate wherein releases and other materials put out by the college will get due coverage, the public relations officer should also try and draw representatives of the press to the campus. It is essential that the media know and understand the college. They cannot gain such knowledge through press releases alone.

Public opinion leaders are often cited as an important public. It is difficult to define what such a leader is, or what may be included in such a public. Often professional people who take a more-than-passing interest in civic affairs become leaders. Editorialists, columnists, and radio and TV commentators fit into the group. So do some politicians. The job of the public relations office with respect to this specific public is to make certain that these people understand the institution, that they find ways to relate to it, and that they talk about it positively. It is perhaps needless to stress again that what these people say will often be echoed by other larger audiences.

For most postsecondary educational institutions, various levels of government will figure importantly as specific audiences for the public relations effort. The states are taking on a greater share of the financing obligation for such institutions as the community colleges, technical institutes, and vocational schools. The federal government will be expected to share more significantly in the educational burden in future years. Of course, many community colleges receive substantial support from local government.

Each of these government sectors could be, and in the end must be, considered as separate audiences for the institution.

For the public relations effort, this means (1) a certain amount of lobbying, (2) being thoroughly acquainted with the wide array of federal programs through which support can be obtained, (3) making certain that all levels of government are aware of and understand the institution, and (4) seeing that proposals get proper consideration. At the state level, of course, the college, either united with other institutions of the same kind or individually, will need to curry support of legislators to make certain, first that bills are passed that favor all education and second that omnibus bills emerging from legislation will give a fair share to each kind of educational institution. For years, community colleges and other types of two-year post-secondary educational units did not get a fair share of support from education bills at both state and federal levels. There is competition for both the state and federal dollar—friendly, perhaps, but there.

One of the problems that has plagued community colleges with regard to federal funding programs has been inability to come up with imaginative programs, or once having come up with such programs, inability to express them or present them in such a way as to get the desired bureaucratic approvals. Staffing has been discussed in another chapter. Here again is evidence of the need for full staffing with competent, qualified people who understand the development process and can express the interests and concerns of the college in clear, concise, and intelligent terms. Moreover, public relations personnel must include federal and state offices on their beats. It is not enough to know the legislators, to call on representatives. Once legislation is passed and funds are appropriated, the control of

funding moves to the desks of the bureaucrats, so it is vital
to know the bureau and section heads and to become
acquainted with and monitor the processes that eventually
lead to the support for the institution and its programs.

It is also essential that the public relations office make
every effort to see to it that personnel of the institution
are represented on state committees and even on national
advisory groups* that will ultimately decide how the pie is
divided. Too often in the past, community colleges went
unrepresented on committees that were actually determining their fate.

Public schools obviously form another important specific audience for community colleges. They are the source
of many of the students, particularly the younger people,
who will eventually turn up on community college campuses. Secondary school people often consider the community
college last. Counselors and teachers, generally having come
out of four-year colleges, still tend to think in terms of the
big university or the state college as the next step. The
public relations office must apply the same techniques, and
even make special efforts through publications, speeches,
exhibits, and meetings with high school people at the
college, to put the community college first rather than last.

Four-year colleges and universities constitute another
body that is crucial to the community college. Too often,
the two seem to be at arms length. Jealousy and competition are pervasive. Yet, universities are increasingly dependent upon the work of the community colleges for their
well-being, and certainly community colleges must be able
to hold out the promise of transfer to many of their
students. The community college public relations office can

---

*The National Council for Resource Development, to be discussed later, is
contributing to improvement of relations with federal and state governments.

serve as a catalyst in bringing such situations to the attention of other members of the administrative team and can come up with materials and approaches to bridge the public relations gap. One important approach is for university and community college public relations officers to spend some time together and try to work out public relations plans that will be to their mutual advantage. Community colleges and other forms of postsecondary institutions at less than the four-year level have come out of the shadows of the universities and four-year colleges. They no longer—if they ever did—need to apologize or be defensive.

One specific public that most writers dealing with the realm of public relations put at the head of the list is present and prospective donors. Traditionally, however, two-year institutions of higher education, publicly supported, have tended to shy away from solicitation in the private sector. They have assumed, perhaps, that to ask a major corporation or a wealthy individual for assistance is in a sense going to the taxpayers a second time, yet state universities have pursued the big donors for years with great success. They have recognized that there are those who want to have an individual or a personal stake in a particular college or university, and they have not hesitated to call upon that urge. The community colleges which have dared go this route have found it fruitful.

Churches and groups affiliated with religious denominations may often be overlooked in public relations campaigns, on the assumption that these institutions, like community colleges, technical institutions, and private colleges, are looking for support for their own programs and activities. Yet, churches are traditionally associated with education. Many junior colleges, particularly the private institutions which many believe were first to arise of

the postsecondary institutions of two years or less, grew
from the concern of religious denominations for expansion
of education.

Although many denominations have pulled back from
operating colleges themselves or spending heavily to keep
colleges in business, they continue to be an important
public for community-based institutions of postsecondary
education. Good church workers are often those same
people who, if persuaded to do so, will come forward to
assist a college with a particular problem or campaign.
Conversely, a church or group of churches can set up
powerful stumbling blocks in the path of concepts or
curriculums that may be anathema to the religious. Witness
the outcries against sex education in schools or the aboli-
tion of prayer, and other church-related protests. Church
groups command attention in the press; their stands on
issues are widely quoted and documented.

Thus, it behooves the institution to include in its public
relations program special attention to the potential of
church groups as supporters and/or detractors. Church
leaders should be kept posted on college programs and
events; they should be frequently invited to campus. Their
opinions and ideas should be sought on educational programs that might help to uplift the community and bring
about individual fulfillment. It should be kept in mind, too,
that churches often counsel their younger members on
possible educational goals and interests. They should have a
full understanding of the various kinds of educational
options that await young people, including two-year postsecondary institutions, in order to help the youth make
decisions for education. Finally, as postsecondary institutions seek to transplant educational programs from main
campuses to centers in the community, they will often find
excellent facilities available to them at churches—facilities

that would often otherwise go unused for much of the time. Such facilities make ideal centers of outreach, since they are known and used by large bodies of citizens.

Other specific audiences could be called to mind. Certainly, the location of the institution and the type and size of community may dictate to some extent the weight given to each public or the kind of public identified, but in general, the audiences covered here will be typical of those found in almost any community.

To what end does the public relations office concern itself with broad general publics and specific groups? Reck's words still stand as among the best:

> It is, of course, the hope of public relations that every person in a position of leadership will speak up favorably, even enthusiastically. Such a hope has a chance of being realized, however, only if (1) the various contacts between a college and the individuals and groups which form its publics have made a favorable impression, and (2) every effort has been made to interpret fully, accurately and with dignity the objectives, policies and problems of the institution to its many publics. The hope usually has an even greater chance of being realized if members of these publics have been encouraged to speak or act for the institution and have received proper credit and appreciation when they did so. When an institution has perfected its services and relations to the extent outlined above, it invariably finds that members of its publics are, by work and deed, building for it good will far greater than any that could be created through any advertising or publicity it might undertake.*

In short, without friends among the various constituent bodies of a community, the college will fail to have the

---

*W. Emerson Reck, *Public Relations: A Program for Colleges and Universities* (New York: Harper & Row, 1946), pp. 191–192.

kind of influence necessary to carry out its mission.
Indifference and apathy will make it more difficult to
proceed, and outright opposition at every step of the way
can bring the learning process to a slow and unpleasant
state.

IS REACHING OTHER PUBLICS THE JOB
OF PUBLIC RELATIONS ALONE?

The preceding discussion conjures up the image of a
public relations office constantly in session, vigorously
working out blueprints for action with regard to specific
publics. Actually, the well-established program will have
built into it strategies and lines of communication with
various groups. The chief public relations officer, having
come to know the community, will automatically be thinking in terms of the various publics. Other staff will come to
think in the same way, and may develop sensitivities they
can pass on to the chief, who may be preoccupied with
other high-level work. In fact, subordinate staff may
become the conscience for the director or vice-president of
public relations, who in turn performs that function in
relations with other top administrators.

Certainly, many action plans will deal directly with a
specific public or publics. If there seems to be hope of
obtaining support from a particular corporation, then an
action plan will be developed and pursued in connection
with that hope. If the college has a goal of collecting
twenty million dollars in federal support, then a program
will be built to reach that goal. In it, the staff will be
reaching out to a specific public. Meanwhile, every action
plan, every program, will take into account all the publics
and how they may react to a particular public relations
plan. There may be those publics, or a public in the

community, that is actually opposed to federal support, for example. That fact will be considered and dealt with as the public relations office seeks money from Washington.

While cultivating support of specific publics, there should be awareness of the need for balance in that support. Just as politicians are sometimes accused of being tools of this or that group, so can an institution of postsecondary education. This is an ever-present problem. There are obviously individuals, often representing large sectors of the community, who seem to have more time, energy, and inclination to take an active role in the program of the institution. Obviously, such participation cannot be discouraged, but the public relations office will need to put forth greater effort to insure that other groups and individuals are equally well represented.

Much of the work of a public relations office with regard to the external publics is outgoing. Its concern will be to place appropriate materials and information in the hands of specific groups, or of the leaders of such groups. It will need to go to individuals and their constituencies. It will spend a good deal of time in the state capital when the legislature is in session. It will monitor the Washington government departments and provide a flow of worthwhile proposals. For many groups and individuals, the only way to reach them is to take the message to them.

Again, the stress in this book is on participation and involvement. Representatives of the publics that we expect to support the institution must see it and feel it to believe it. You can fill the ears of a newspaper reporter or a foundation representative with a tremendous array of information, but the same message can be gotten across, more resoundingly in most cases, when the individual being solicited is at the institution.

As an employee of a national organization representing

a large segment of postsecondary education, I was called upon to write many articles and prepare many publications dealing with the wonders of the institutions. Much of what I wrote had to be assimilated from reports and releases coming from the institutions themselves, but frequently I was able to go out to campuses and to gather the necessary material, call on the right people, and do interviews upon which stories could be based. Needless to say, those visits gave me the feeling and spirit that could not be obtained through statistical reports and analyses coming via the mails. The articles that I then wrote and submitted were far more meaningful, had more feeling, were more accurate, and, last but most important, got better play in the media.

Far too many articles, far too many speeches have been given on the subject of community colleges by people who have little or no exposure to the institutions themselves. Among the leading writers on community colleges, for example, have been learned professors from four-year colleges and universities. Often critical, such articles led one to suspect that the writer had at most visited one campus and talked to three people. The same is true of national media. In a national TV report on private higher education, the commentator dismissed in passing the whole community college sector when he said most were no better than a good high school. Obviously, that commentator had no first-hand knowledge of the community college. His was a gratuitous remark, based on his own impression, that might better have gone unsaid since it had no foundation in fact.

National media attention will be treated later in this book, the point that the real story that community colleges and other two-year institutions want told can come only from experience with and exposure to the institutions. Without such exposure, the teller of the story will never be able to make a public truly understand it. It cannot be conveyed through press releases and publications alone;

involvement and participation are absolutely necessary. It is clear that a great deal depends upon personal contact. The question is how a two- or three-person public relations staff can be personally involved with thousands of people, representing a great variety of publics. Obviously, the office staff cannot do that, nor can it even maintain constant contact with the leaders of the various groups, though there are some that it will be dealing with on a day-to-day basis—newspapers, state legislators, broadcasters, state and federal agencies, and some corporations that are especially interested or involved in the institution. But if the office has done its job well within the immediate family, then it can depend on many of these contacts to be secured and maintained through other members of the family. The community service division staff will be in day-to-day contact with churches, social groups, and community agencies as it divines programming needs and sets up appropriate activities to meet those needs. Occupational education personnel will be making and maintaining appropriate contacts with labor groups, business, and industry, involving representatives of these groups in advisory capacities, as part-time teachers, and as facilitators of the occupational education process. The president and other top administrators will be involved in community activities that will reach community leadership at all levels. Student leaders and counselors will make their impact felt spreading their impressions and perceptions of the institution.

The point to be emphasized here is that the contacts of the other members of the family will not always occur automatically. Impetus must come from the public relations office, in some instances, to bring about the contacts. The public relations office must also be constantly on the alert to be sure that what is being passed between groups within the college and those without is appropriate, accurate, fair, and honest.

Guidelines for Chapter 6 _____

The need for concern with both general and specific publics within the broad segments of the community cannot be overstated. Not only is this concern necessary to assure an effective public relations program; it can result in more efficient, more objective, and better-targeted action plans. A sharply focused public relations program will have in mind a specific public or publics, as well as the general community climate. Some guidelines:

1. The community college, or other type of two-year postsecondary publicly supported institution, can be said to be in and of the community; therefore it is concerned with the total community. Public relations functionaries will constantly be concerned with overall public opinion.
2. However, for long-range planning, the public relations office may find its job more workable by looking at broad segments of the general public such as professionals, labor, business and industry, ethnic groups. (Though minorities will also be found in other publics as individuals, in jobs, and in professions, they also become a special public in the context of their own culture.)
3. The public relations office can be more effective and efficient when it breaks down the broad segments

into more specific audiences. It must be sensitive to reactions of the specific groups to college activities and programs, and it will find it prudent to give special attention to those reactions.

4. The public relations office will create a climate of cooperation among other institutional officers that will take the burden of direct contact with many specific publics off public relations personnel, but it is important that other staff members discharge their responsibilities with sensitivity to public relations overtones.

5. While much of the public relations work is of necessity outgoing in nature, effort must be extended to bring specific audiences to the institution and to involve representatives in college or school activities so that impressions will be formed that are based on direct contact with the college and its family.

6. The public relations staff constitute the consciences of the college. It will be their function to know all the various publics and be sensitive to their concerns and issues. They will convey these concerns to other administrators and college leaders, making certain that they are mindful of the implications and repercussions that particular college actions might have on a special public or group of publics.

7. Community colleges and other public postsecondary educational institutions should recognize that there will be individuals and small groups, such as corporate bodies, that will be willing and interested in contributing to the institution. Special efforts should be made to cultivate such individuals and/or groups.

8. Action plans should be developed which focus on certain publics where the response or contribution of

a specific audience is essential to a particular goal. A carefully worked out and strategized approach to a state legislature on a particular educational bill might constitute such a plan.

9. The college, with its public relations staff as conscience, should guard against any group that might have too great an influence on college decisions. Proper planning will make certain that there is well-balanced representation from the many specific publics in activities and campaigns that may emerge or be planned.

Special Problems and Tasks _____ 7

"*I want you to know,*" *the caller said,* "*that I have a statement here by Professor Jones in which he announces his resignation under duress. Can you confirm the resignation?*" *The caller was a newspaper editor, and the question was addressed to the college public relations vice-president.*

"*Yes, I believe that he has unofficially resigned, although we had hoped that he would want to make some kind of joint announcement. I am surprised that he would go directly to you.*"

"*That's why I am calling,*" *the editor said,* "*to give you a chance to talk with the professor. He has said some very nasty things about the college and perhaps will want to soften the statement before we go to press with it. It will probably do him more harm than it will do the college.*"

The above dialogue contains a couple of interesting points with regard to public relations. First, it shows that this public relations office has done its job well in building close rapport with the local newspaper. The fact that the editor called and was concerned that the statement of resignation would be harmful both to the college and the individual demonstrates that a climate of good feeling and concern had been built up with this important audience. Second, it clearly illustrates how various audiences turn to the public relations office for the amelioration of problems. It was assumed by the newspaper editor that the public relations officer would have access to the professor, and that the professor might listen to him.

In this particular real-life incident, the public relations officer did have that kind of relationship. He was able to do what no other person could do—persuade the professor to change his statement, to eschew some of the harsh criticisms that he had made. Though this is an isolated incident of a sort that should not often arise, it does illustrate that the public relations officer and staff are at the center of life at the college. If they performed capably, they will be more than just strategists for special programs and campaigns; they will be in the eye of the storms. Their jobs go far beyond the routine. The specialist who attempts to isolate himself from the crises or pawn responsibility for the bond election off onto some other office will not be an effective member of the management team.

Though the public relations staff may have excellent rapport with the press, as in the illustration above, they will nonetheless be in the cross fire when the press, as it sooner or later will, aims its big guns of criticism at a particular program or policy. That will happen no matter how much careful planning goes into the establishment of good relations with the media. More often than not, the criticism may be well-founded. Undesirable as such circumstances may be, far worse is the situation in which a particular newspaper, radio station, or TV outlet seems actually to have a generalized grudge against an institution. Some program developed in the past, some obscure affront to a publisher, some unknown element may be at the root of such a calamitous situation. Fortunately, the kind of personal journalism that in the past was too often characteristic of the media has in large part disappeared. Nonetheless, it must figure into any discussion of the responsibilities of the public relations office.

This chapter, then, deals with some of the special problems of the public relations office, both the good and the bad. A bond election presents special problems and challenges. A bad press presents a special problem. A student protest presents a special problem. So do faculty dismissals and recruitment of students. Receipt of private support may present special problems for some institutions. Sometimes several such problems arise almost simultaneously. Protests and criticism cannot be programmed—although many come in the midst of a major fund campaign. In fact, they may result from that campaign. The press may not recognize the need, or it may be critical of the approach. Students may protest against an effort that they don't understand or some college program that they don't feel is necessary. These seeming disparate problems do fit together and constitute a major part of the whole of public relations. They put pressures on the public relations staff that may often seem beyond the call of duty.

PRESS CRITICISM OR NEGATIVISM

Dealing with the press is something of an art, something of a gift. It is a vital but routine part of the job of the public relations staff. Generally, if that job is carried out faithfully and well, the press will be favorable and supportive of most activities and policies of the institution. It will certainly open its pages to reports and statements issued by the public relations office on routine developments and day-to-day activities. It will carry objective articles about the development of new facilities, the adding of new curriculums, and the doings of faculty and students. But the press also has an obligation to question and probe, to go behind the scenes of some college actions that may appear to be questionable. It may do so as the result of some questions by other publics, or it may simply find that a particular college program or event does not meet with its

philosophy of what education should be. If its probings and
investigations turn up evidence that supports its skepticism
or concerns about a particular policy of action, then those
concerns will be expressed on the editorial pages of the
newspapers and in commentary by radio and TV broadcasters.

In most cases, the institution, through its public relations office, will be able to anticipate in advance that a
particular action may be controversial and subject to criticism. Obviously, if the institution, its administration, and
trustees have made up their minds that the proposed action
will advance the mission, that the arguments for it are
incontrovertible, then it will be announced and implement-
ed. Many steps that must be taken in institutional planning
will in the long run have to survive adverse public and press
reaction.

On the other hand, there may infrequently be a planned action that might be delayed or avoided altogether
because the anticipated negative response far outweighs
whatever advantage or benefit may be expected. It may fall
to the public relations officer, in his policy-making role, to
oppose such an action on the basis of its possible adverse
reaction. The question of the location of a satellite campus
was used earlier as an example, and it can serve again here.
The public relations officer may sense, or his intelligence
sources may tell him, that this decision will not only be
unpopular, but in fact, inappropriate.

Once the decision about a particular program or activity
becomes inevitable, then the public relations office must
swing into action. Anticipating press criticism, it must open
all channels to insure that the issue is put in perspective. If
possible, the press should be taken into the confidence of
chief administrators prior to the announcement of the
decision. It should be given the opportunity, in fact the

outright encouragement, to talk with trustees, administrators, and others involved in the forthcoming decision. The financial records on the subject should be open to the press. Every effort should be made to allay suspicions and skepticism in advance. The matter must be treated as openly, and with as little red tape showing, as possible.

The cardinal principles of good public relations—honesty, fairness, accuracy—ought to be brought into play. If the facts are made clear and the channels of communication are kept open, then at least the criticism will be more objective and less voluble and violent. If newspapers and broadcasting media can be persuaded to say, "We think it's a bad policy (or an inappropriate action), but we will wait to see how it works out in the end," then the public relations effort will have been worthwhile; something will have been accomplished. In some cases, no amount of planning and effort will alleviate the criticism, but at the very least, the press relations officer can, if she has done her job at all well, hope to obtain coverage of the college viewpoint as well as of the opposition viewpoint. Though she can never demand, she can plead her case before the editors in hopes that all viewpoints will be presented. That much can usually be won.

There are some kinds of cases the college cannot win. If, for example, there has been malfeasance in a particular office or unwise decisions have been made and announced, the college and its public relations office may have to take its lumps. It will simply have to endure the questioning and criticism that is due. If possible, of course, the public relations office will again try to communicate freely, open doors to information and background data, be honest and accurate. While such an approach may not set well with some of those involved in whatever unpleasant situation exists, it will in the long run be better for the institution.

Nothing should be hidden from the press—and usually it cannot be anyway. We are dealing with public institutions which depend upon public dollars and a public trust. Some criticism must simply be met head on and there is no way to plan for it.

FUND DRIVES

Most institutions of postsecondary education are constantly in pursuit of the essential, vital dollar. Whether the institution is private, public, or proprietary, it will be engaged in various programs and efforts designed to keep the institution solvent and to allow it to plan for the future. If it has a well-organized public relations and development program as a part of the management machinery, a major goal of that operation will be to insure acquisition of funding from year to year. The term *support* has been used constantly in the foregoing chapters. Gaining it is a large part of the development work. Creation of good will not only fills classrooms but generates the funding needed to build and expand classrooms and other facilities.

Obviously, if the institution depends primarily on student tuitions and fees, then its program of public relations will include great emphasis on recruitment of people who can pay the tuition and fees. The college that is dependent upon state monies will aim its fund raising program at the state legislature and state offices responsible for allocation of support. The institution that looks to the private dollar will concentrate on reaching foundations, corporations, individuals, and alumni. All institutions today will also be looking at federal possibilities. Most will be concentrating on a mixture of these publics, perhaps pouring a greater degree of its fund-raising strength into an effort with one or two special publics. In short, the acquiring of funding is never missing from the public relations picture, perhaps somewhat unfortunately when one considers that the main thrust of an educational institution ought to be learning. Alas, learning cannot take place without teachers, modern equipment, and some kind of facilities (even storefronts cost something to maintain). It is unlikely that the need to raise funds will lessen in the foreseeable future; in fact, it is likely to occupy more, rather than less, college personnel time in the decades ahead.

But most institutions have times when a special development effort is needed. It may be a long-range general development campaign calling for the raising of multimillion dollars within a given period, or it may be, as often is the case with community colleges that receive major support from a local community, a "quick and dirty" effort to pass a special bond election. Whatever the special effort or kind of institution, similar techniques, communications devices, public relations ploys, and people are involved. A multimillion dollar campaign may require a more sophisticated approach and result in the employment of outside counsel and assistance, while the special election will normally rely primarily on the tools and people at hand. But fund raising is fund raising. Certain techniques and tools are brought into play. Action plans are developed. Goals are communicated in detail. The driving force behind such campaigns and efforts is a go-for-broke attitude, what the pundits in times of war call the "all-out effort."

In any such campaign, the communications office and other elements of management should address themselves to the following questions before developing and organizing the campaign:

1. What kind of climate is there for a special campaign? Is the community or special public ready for an effort that will eventually cost them where it hurts most?
2. If the climate is not right, if the community is not predisposed, yet the need is so great as to require the campaign anyway, what can be done to change the situation and attitudes? What ingredients will be put into the mixture to try and overcome an unfavorable climate?
3. What should be a realistic goal for the campaign, in terms of dollars? Has adequate groundwork been laid by communicating the need? What new communications efforts will be needed?
4. Are the power sources (media, politicians, civic groups, corporate leaders) attuned to the needs of the campaign? What will their attitudes be? Particularly, are the media in the fold?
5. Can members of the immediate college family, as well as those close to it in the community, be counted on to lend moral and physical support to the campaign? Will they lend their strength and leadership to the communications effort that will be required?

If the answers to most of these questions turns out to be negative, then perhaps the effort should be postponed or delayed until the climate changes, and the climate must be changed by good public relations that will overcome the negative situation that exists. It would indeed be unwise to go forward in the face of what would seem to constitute total opposition. Sometimes the need or the problem may be so great that the program will have to be launched anyway. Those responsible will find then it necessary to look for and capitalize on that "reservoir of community respect" that John Dunn speaks of: "A campaign for public support can rarely be successful if there does not exist a reservoir of community respect for the value of the colleges in question. That reservoir exists in the communities served by the Foothill District's DeAnza and Foothill Colleges."*

The article in which Dunn was quoted traced a successful financial election in support of the Foothill District in California. That District won its election, while nine others failed, at a time when voters in California and elsewhere had demonstrated growing reluctance to support community colleges or any kind of educational institution. How the district did it provides a case in point for this treatise. Following, paraphrased, are some highlights of that case as reported by Ruth Durst of the public relations staff.

First of all, the college faced up to the fact that it was not a good time to seek increased taxes of the citizens. In fact, it was a bad time and the district said so, in restrained but factual copy in advertisements placed in local media. The copy is worth repeating:

> It's a bad year to ask for a tax increase. But we can't wait. Our community colleges, DeAnza and Foothill, are in trouble. Right now. The budget for operating the colleges has not increased in proportion to the growth of enrollment—66 percent in the last five years—accompanied by a 26 percent increase in the cost of operating as the result of inflation. Proposition "s" is intended simply to maintain the status quo; to maintain the present quality of education. It asks for an increase in the operational

*John Dunn, quoted in Ruth Durst, "Foothill: A Financial Winner in California," *Community and Junior College Journal*, December-January 1972–1973, p. 22.

tax rate of ten cents per $100 assessed valuation for the next
four years. The net tax increase, however, will be less than ten
cents. Passage of Proposition "s" will allow a cutback in various
restricted taxes and will mean only about five cents per $100
additional, or an added $3.75 a year on a $30,000 home.*

The district had begun its efforts early and done its
homework well. A year before the election, in October,
1971, the district had appointed a community committee
of 150 (making for an augmented board) to make a study
of its financial problems and to help develop a finance
recommendation. To insure credibility, the study committee included representatives of the Taxpayers Rebellion
and the United Taxpayers Association (area protest groups).
That augmented board recommended the election of a
ten-cent tax increase for a four-year term commencing July
1, 1972.

Even with that green light, Durst points out, the college
hesitated, using another ploy before actually calling for an
election. It used the time to soften the media and other
publics, including minority groups and community organizations. Eventually, the climate was judged right for the
controversial election, and the machinery was put into
motion for the campaign with the establishment of a
campaign organization that included logistics, finance, publications and the media, and a general campaign committee.
A steering committee composed of staff, students, and
adminstrators coordinated activities. Common techniques
were used: advertising, stories in the papers, discussions
with community leaders, issuance of reports, but this
well-organized group also came up with new ideas. For
example, it sought successfully to gain voter registration for
the eighteen- to twenty-year old group, recognizing that

*Durst, *ibid.*

such a new voter segment would probably be on the side of the college. They went to the community for money to pay for the campaign and raised $36,115. They called on professionals for volunteer work. The publications and media committee were able to obtain the services of copy writers and layout artists to develop a series of newspaper advertisements. Some three hundred volunteers rang doorbells to press the cause. They distributed and used in advertisements testimonials from satisfied customers (former students), and they attempted to answer in copy the most difficult questions about such matters as student radicalism, declining school enrollments, and physical ecucation facilities.

Direct mail pieces geared to the interests of special publics were continually distributed to them. Mailings to business and industry, for example, contained the strong economic argument of a ten million dollar district payroll accomodated with a fifteen million-dollar-plus budget, most of it spent locally, with only sixty percent raised from local taxes.

The district took advantage of the unexpected. Fortuitously, the Accreditation Commission of the Western Association of Schools and Colleges issued a preliminary report (it had been reviewing routinely the accreditation of the college) just before the election. It strongly recommended Foothill College, and stressed its "critical and crucial" need for financial support.

Foothill District won its campaign, not by an overwhelming margin, but it was a victory, nonetheless. It is inescapably clear that it could not have done so, in the face of a generally poor climate, had it not brought into play the kind of sophisticated public relations techniques that involves the community—both internal and external. Here was a campaign that (1) relied on careful, long-range advance planning, (2) foresaw opposition and early on

involved those who might be opposed, (3) made certain
that elements of the community deemed essential to the
successful outcome were on the side of the college before
an election was called for, (4) took advantage of fortuitous
circumstances, such as the accrediting commission's report,
(5) made excellent use of the members of the college
family, (6) came up with new campaign ideas, (7) faced
issues head on, (8) utilized professionals in the community
for help in the campaign, (9) was able to conduct a special
financial campaign while simultaneously maintaining the
overall campaign, and (10) it tailored appeals and messages
for special publics.

Here, in short, was a district with a relatively small
public relations staff that employed techniques and used
tools that would put many professional fund-raising organizations to shame. What Foothill District did could be used
as a model in any kind of campaign, with obvious changes
and refinements to suit other conditions in other communities. Moreover, think what the district could have done
had there been a favorable climate from the start. But just
as the Foothill planners did, most postsecondary institutions should deal from a hand that is not loaded to begin
with and consider the battle ahead as one requiring hard-
hitting, well-organized planning.

Some will raise the question "How can such a plan or
program be translated into a campaign to raise support
from the private sector? My institution cannot go to a total
community—a body of taxpayers—to acquire the funding
that it needs." In this different kind of situation, the tools
and techniques to be used are similar. In general, the
overall effort will have the same goal: to convince certain
publics that this institution needs support, that it is deserving of support, and that it has a contribution to make. The
campaign will normally be of longer duration and the

financial goal will be higher. The effort will involve identifying for approach specific corporations and foundations (those that may be particularly attuned to the type of institution and its programs and concerns), as well as blocks of individuals (such as alumni), and within those blocks, segments that can be expected to go beyond average giving and come up with the big donations.

Once the potential donors have been identified, then strategies, perhaps on a broader geographical basis, will be developed along the lines of those of the Foothill District special campaign. Obviously, prominent board members, the president, and leading friends of the institution, will be used in making personal calls on corporations and on foundations, as well as on other potential big donors. Special mailings and reports will be used to prepare the way for the direct appeals that must take place. The media will perhaps be less important in this kind of campaign, although some effort should be expended on placement of articles that can be used to support the cause. Such an effort might be concentrated on professional or semiprofessional national organizations.

In this kind of effort, the institution might be more likely to use an outside fund-raising agency. College personnel and associates may logically be expected to carry out the legwork, but the counsel might help chart the total plan and recommend approaches and strategies. But the goal remains the same: to generate needed support and assistance from identified publics and groups, as well as individuals.

RECRUITMENT OF STUDENTS

In recent years, the word *recruitment* has reentered the lexicon of the advancement team at most postsecondary institutions of higher education. During the boom years for enrollment in the 1950s and 60s, except in the case of some of the private institutions, both four-year and two-year, the word had almost disappeared from the language. There were more students to go around than all of America's colleges and universities could accomodate. The escalation in the planning of new community colleges and technical institutes can be traced in part to limitations placed on entry by many four-year colleges and universities. When the boom was on, the mere statement of facts in a college brochure may have been enough. A pass at local high schools was sufficient to remind students of the availability of the community college. If they didn't take the bait, so what? The institution was bursting at the seams anyway.

A significant plank in the mission platforms of many two-year institutions of higher education has been to try and reach "all who can benefit from some kind of postsecondary experience." Most conscientiously looked for ways to expand citizens' horizons; such terms as *storefront* education and *outreach* became euphemisms for extension of college programs. But this was not recruitment in the real sense, because it did not involve a need to fill classrooms. Plans based on projected student enrollments in a given community were often far outdated when the institutions opened to overflowing capacity. It was a bear market for all higher education, as the new concept of open-door education was accepted by the millions.

Yet, statistics show that all Americans are not being reached. Millions still have little or no opportunity for education, or believe that they don't. Even the availability of inexpensive education is not enough to attract them. Or they are not aware of its availability. Even many of those who can afford some kind of postsecondary education are turned off, disinterested, apathetic about going on after high school.

Public relations departments must work on recruitment in tandem with other affected administrative arms—especially counseling and admissions—which are inescapably involved in recruitment. It is both a practical and a moral issue. First, to be accountable and obtain the support it must have to offer quality education, the institution must show that it is serving ever-increasing numbers of people, even now, at a time when support by some states is being curtailed. Second (perhaps first in order of importance), the institution, following the mandate laid down for it, must serve all the different kinds of people it can. If college-age young people are staying away in large droves and not being served elsewhere, then some questions have to be raised about the viability of the institution's programs and the effectiveness of its public relations program. If opportunities for people who desperately need the kind of help that can only be provided by education are going begging, then additional questions may be asked. Expansion into other areas—such as programs for the aging, for women, or for training in factories—ought also to be pursued, though such new programs cannot substitute for educating the young men and women who will take their places as the bulwark of society in future decades.

What it all means is that recruitment must become more public-relations oriented. Rather than rely on a computerized operation that churns out numbers and data, the public relations effort must play up some of the side benefits of education, even some of the more fun things, if you will. In the past, most recruitment has been aimed at parents who often were critical of anything that suggested their money would be going for anything other than good, hard education. More and more young people today are on their own at age eighteen—by choice. They often pay a large share of the cost of their education, either through earnings from part-time and summer jobs or through loans and grants. This means that the recruitment effort, while not ignoring parents, must also get under the skins of the young people themselves.

Publications, press information, TV spots, high school programs, special events should all be used in reaching potential students. Community colleges and other localized schools have to reckon today with an unusual phenomenon: It was once thought that those who could benefit from the local institution would do so because they could not afford to go anywhere else or would be unacceptable to some other college or university, but today, in an era of virtually complete mobility, young people often can go where they please and are sought after by many four-year colleges and universities. So the community college public relations program has to demonstrate that there are some justifiable reasons for taking the first two years locally.

The best public relations program won't completely solve the recruitment problem, but if it stresses (1) the educational strengths of the institution, (2) the good life and the side benefits the college offers, (3) the kind of personal and human relationships that can be developed and sustained, and (4) the job rewards that will come from the college experience, then it will have a better chance of success. Young people, although mobile, have many uncertainties; a convincing recruitment-public relations effort may help to erase them.

Recruitment, in a sense, is simply a part of the ongoing public relations program. The same message that might help to insure passage in the state legislature of a bill in support of a college or system of colleges may have meaning for young people. It may have to be tailored differently, packaged more attractively and promotionally for the student. It comes back to publics. The way a message is told to one public may not properly influence another. There are different strokes for different people, and the public relations program must take that into account.

In terms of tools and techniques, the public relations office should use brighter approaches. Here are some ideas, a composite of techniques used by a number of institutions:

1. Do far more work on school campuses—and better and more interesting work. Rather than rely merely on a counselor's little speech, or a handful of brochures, make certain that those who do the work go in with lively materials that will attract and hold attention. One of the best techniques today is multimedia—the combining of music (which might be hard rock) with lively pictures and film to create highlights of the college in a manner for the teen-age audience.

2. Get the cooperation of schools in bringing more school groups to campus—then do something exciting. If it takes a rock concert, then lace the usual tour with such a program. Put on special events that will attract young people to the campus of their own accord, rather than wait for an organized School Day visit.

3. Save the hard-headed message for parents. Play up in direct mail what this institution can do for the young person. Make it difficult for the parent to resist.

4. Use the testimonial approach; it is effective with young people. The tone should be, "Man, this place is cool."

5. Get the college students into the act. Nothing new about that, but it deserves emphasis. They are the best ambassadors with young people who, after all, are virtually their contemporaries.

6. Make an effort to get a student-related column in a local newspaper. Most colleges have one or more young people who can write, and most papers are open to columns which they can get for little or nothing.

7. Make certain that college newspapers are made available in schools and other public places. While the newspaper may sometimes be controversial, it does reflect more or less accurately the spirit and life style of a campus.

8. In appeals to minority groups, attempt to speak their language. Produce materials in Spanish, if necessary, for large Spanish-speaking groups. Don't be afraid to use the language of the ghetto or the barrio so long as it does not appear to come across as a put-on. The word is *communicate*, by whatever means necessary.

9. Get out the old brass drum. Beat it loudly. Recruitment provides opportunity to use the latent press agentry that exists in most public relations people. Have fun.

10. If this is a community-based institution, then make certain it comes off as such. The message should be loud and clear in whatever the means of communication.

Of course all that has been suggested here does not fall upon the beleaguered public relations office; much of the work of recruitment will be carried out by another office or offices. But because recruitment is contact with people, public relations has a guiding role to play in how it is organized and carried out. As in other areas, the public relations office has a responsibility to see that this work is done well and right.

THE FOUNDATION

Some public institutions of postsecondary education find that accepting financial support creates problems and burdens. Laws may mitigate against the receipt of funds from corporations, individuals, and even private foundations. Such regulations have retarded advancement programs in some places. The reasoning of those responsible for such regulations seems to be that a college that relies on public, tax-dollar support, has no right to go back to the public again for additional funds except via duly constituted bond elections.

Community colleges have worked within these regulations where they apply by establishing their own private foundations, and some others have established foundations because they provide mere flexibility in fund raising. Such foundations, organized as corporate bodies, are set up to receive donations from individuals and corporations and in most cases actively solicit such support. These tax-exempt organizations may be closely tied to the college by personnel and governance, although they are more effective if operated under their own governing board and/or personnel.

Woodbury makes these observations about the advantages of the private foundation:

> Besides assisting in soliciting the private dollar in the community, a community college foundation has other advantages. It can lease certain college facilities, such as the bookstore or cafeteria,

and then own and operate it. Thus, the profits go to the foundation to be managed by it and dispersed in a manner that might not be possible otherwise.

The foundation can also own land and lease it to the college if there are legal restrictions placed upon the college on the amount of land to be held, or if there are sensitivities in the community to the college's physical expansion and acquisition of property.*

In essence, such a foundation can do for institutions of postsecondary education what many cannot do for themselves in terms of raising, receiving, and using monies. If such machinery is necessary for gaining additional support, then the college should put energy and substance into setting it up. There is absolutely no reason why a community college or any other institution of postsecondary education should not actively seek additional support, particularly from the private sector. As Woodbury notes, "Its [the foundation's] success ... is dependent upon the time and energies available on the part of the college staff and their ability to select enthusiastic board members and to maintain their interest. It should only be created when the college is willing to give it a high priority, adequate staff, and a commitment of institutional resources; otherwise there is more to be lost than to be gained."†

In most situations, the privately organized foundation should have its own board of nine to fifteen members which would also include the president of the college or school as an ex officio member. At least one other representative of the institution should serve on the board, and the entire board should be organized by the institution.

*Kenneth B. Woodbury, "Community College Foundation," *Community and Junior College Journal,* December–January 1972–1973, p. 16.
†*Ibid.*

Because it is not usually an elected group, the college can have the last word on who is appointed. After all, if the foundation is to be a fund-raising mechanism for the institution, then it is to be expected that the board will be selected carefully to provide the prestige, the clout, and the names that will be respected by those likely to donate to the college. In short, it should contain people who can open doors and have an impact on fund raising or in developing programs that will assist the college beyond its normal budgeting activity.

The board should generally operate under the wings of the public relations vice-president and the development officer. If the privately organized foundation is the main source or receptacle for resources, then a considerable amount of the time of the development man will be budgeted to the foundation. It may mean, of course, that his salary will be divided between the regular college budget and that of the foundation. In cases in which development activities are not so restricted—but where a foundation may be desirable because of the availability of some private dollars that otherwise could not be solicited—there may be need for a special staff. Even in such cases, direction should come from the institution.

Charles County Community College in Maryland has a private foundation in which it uses a special board and a part-time executive who reports to the president of the college, who provides overall direction for the foundation and on occasion makes solicitations. The program has limited but reasonable goals. It has been successful. As with all other aspects of college programming, goals are the essential element in determining how the development plan is organized and operated, how it is staffed, how lines of authority are established, and what the direction will be. It is important, however, that the goals of the foundation be consonant with those of the institution for which it exists.

STUDENT PROTESTS, COLLECTIVE BARGAINING, FACULTY DISSENT

The most difficult task of the public relations office is dealing with in-house controversy, whether it be a violent student protest, a heated union-management negotiation, or the dismissal of a popular faculty member on a charge that may leave considerable room for criticism. Even though the public relations office is closely tied to top management of the institution and its chief is represented in the highest levels of administration, the responsible public relations staff should be objective, honest, and straight. They should try to present all sides of a particular controversy, or at least attempt to provide access to all sides, particularly to the press. There are two main responsibilities:

1. Since the chief public relations officer does occupy a position of leadership and does take a part in policy planning and making, he or she should use that position to the utmost to head off the emergence of a bad situation.
2. If the situation does come, then it is up to the public relations officer to provide as much background information as possible to the media, and thus to other publics, and to make appropriate arrangements for coverage on-the-scene where the situation demands that kind of attention.

In meeting the first responsibility, if the public relations office is doing an effective job and keeping in touch with the college community as well as the larger community, it will have ample advance warning of an emerging controversy. It will do everything possible to amass as much background information as it can and take that information to the highest councils of the college. The staff will offer action plans that may help to stave off a violent demonstration or an unpleasant occurrence of some other kind. For example, a beleaguered president, considering the demands of a particular group so outlandish as to not deserve his personal attention, may be persuaded by good public relations advice to change his stance and at least meet with the leadership of the group. Such a meeting may only serve to put off a more unpleasant situation, but there is also always the chance that an eyeball-to-eyeball encounter may result in a resolution of the problem. In some cases, the public relations office may be the middle ground for debate and discussion of certain kinds of issues.

Though anathema to college and school leaders for years, unionism among college personnel is now becoming a fact of life. Collective bargaining is fast becoming as commonplace on the campus as it is in the industrial plant. The role of the public relations officer here is perhaps more obscure than in protests or dissidence, because once the right to bargain is recognized, the duly constituted representatives of institution and personnel play out their own game of public relations. The union more often than not will have its own spokesman; it will churn out its own press releases; it will stage its own press conferences. Instead of representing the total institution, as in most other controversies, the public relations chief will more likely than not be representing a strictly management viewpoint, as he makes available to the press statements presenting the institution's side of the matter. He should, in the interest of harmony, make arrangements for coverage, of the union position, provide access to the college's bargaining event, cooperate with the representative of the union in releasing joint statements, and the like. Much of the process is out of his hands, however, since he will never take an active role in collective bargaining. He cannot deal with the press and at the same time be an agent for the college. He cannot be a negotiator and still fulfill his essential function as the public relations officer.

The public relations officer meets his second responsibility once all efforts to head off a protest have failed. Knowing that there will be press coverage and attention from the media and the public have a right to know what is going on, the public relations officer should take every step possible to insure that there is access to information. In the case of a student protest, for example, he will try to establish lines of communication between student leadership and the press, and of course assist with preparation of statements to be given by the board chairman or the chief administrator expressing the official views of the college. There may even be times when the public relations officer can help the protestors in formulating releases and writing statements that will better reflect their viewpoints. In the process, he may be able to soften or otherwise improve on communications from the dissidents.

A protest or demonstration is a fact of life. Once launched, there is of course hope that it can be ended as soon as possible, but even so, it will be news; it will attract attention. It can not be hidden. It will not go away until energy and time are spent and the issue is resolved. But the college, and the public relations staff, will be there conducting business when it is all over. The public relations staff is out to win friends and influence people, not to make enemies and create an unfavorable climate for the future. Accordingly, it should do its best to be of service during the situation, to bring to bear all its know-how in insuring fair and accurate coverage, and to make certain that the communications process runs smoothly and efficiently, even under the most trying circumstances.

It is true that in recent years there has been a diminution of protests and demonstrations; campuses have become calm. There is no reason, though, to assume that the current complacency will not give way to new waves of dissension. No public relations man or woman who lived through the turbulence of the sixties will ever forget the stresses and strains of that time. None was prepared. There were no guidelines for the public relations role in those conflicts. There will be in the future.

Guidelines for Chapter 7 _____

In this chapter, the special problems or tasks that face all institutions of postsecondary education and have implications for the public relations staff have been explained. Some of these merely have to do with better ways of organizing for better and more effective utilization of resources; others have to do with the unexpected. Still other problems will emerge in the future. There are few existing action plans for handling some of the less pleasant problems that emerge. Though such plans will have to be developed on the spot, here are a few guidelines:

1. Press criticism, or negativism, will occur no matter what steps are taken to avoid it. The public relations office should have the kind of rapport with the press that will insure objective treatment of a situation, even if the press is inherently in opposition.
2. Honesty, fairness, and accuracy will serve the public relations office best in cases where there may be negative reaction from the press.
3. Launching of special fund campaigns should take place only when (1) there is a favorable public attitude toward the need for such an effort and/or (2) when there is no other way out.
4. Once a special fund campaign is decided upon, it should be an all-out effort calling upon all the

sources for people and ideas that can be mustered. Months of careful advance planning should precede the actual effort.

5. Recruitment is a special task for some postsecondary institutions of higher education. New appeals are needed to suit the new life styles and the mobility of today's society.

6. For many public institutions restricted by state laws, it may be necessary or desirable to establish a foundation to receive private and other support. Its establishment may bring needed funding for projects that might not otherwise see the light of day.

7. Private foundations should be conducted under the general direction of the public relations or development office.

8. Public relations staff have a two-fold role with regard to distasteful demonstrations on campus: to try and head off expected dissidence, but when that is not possible, to serve as a conduit for objective and accurate information about the issues involved.

9. With regard to unionism and collective bargaining, the public relations office should help to insure the free flow of information to various publics concerned. It should not take an active role in negotiations for either side.

Beyond
the Local Scene _____ 8

CBS veteran news commentator Eric Sevareid, reporting from China during President Nixon's visit to that country in 1970, discussed a visit to Peking University. He was not much impressed. He likened the university to an American junior college, and not in a flattering way. His comment reached millions via television and was also quoted in Time *and other national magazines.*

Even the gangster types peopling Robin Moore's bestselling The Fifth Estate, *which deals with crime as a business, have a low opinion of two-year colleges (an opinion which is obviously a reflection of the author's understanding of them). One of the characters in the book, a crime leader, refers to them as "half-assed community colleges."*

More often than not, nationally prominent persons in the media, whose stray comments in a book, newspaper, or on television have tremendous impact on attitudes toward postsecondary education, are disdainful of any kind of educational enterprise that deviates from the traditional and the conventional. Their attitudes reflect lack of knowledge and appreciation of or interest in the "new" forms of postsecondary education. Their low (or no) opinion of community colleges, junior colleges, technical institutes, and vocationally-oriented schools, may also reflect a lack of any real public relations effort by the institution aimed at changing the national climate of opinion. This lack of public relations effort probably stems from lack of concern,

or perhaps apathy, about the importance of gaining favorable attention beyond the local community. If the colleges
are not serving people beyond the town or county they
are established to serve, then why go national? It is without
doubt a questionable matter. Why should a college or
institute—a local educational unit—be concerned about
national views and impressions that will probably not have
any immediate impact on the institution's fate or future?
Why should the public relations budget be spread even
thinner to try and cover statewide, let alone the national
media? After all, most of the dollars and students are at
home. That's where the fires of support, interest, and
appreciation should be kept burning.

Assuming that there is a modicum of interest in generating state, regional, and national attention for postsecondary institutions of higher education of less than four
years, other questions arise. How can this institution, a
community college, hope to compete with the Ivy League
and the other great universities for national attention?

THE REASONS WHY

While it is true that the primary responsibility of an
institution is to the particular geographic area it is set up to
serve, it should not overlook the effects that opinion
leaders far beyond that locale can have. Their favorable
statements about the institution will more often than not
help to generate local pride and enthusiasm and result in
even greater support in the community. People like to see
their town or their community on the map, so long it is
shown in a favorable light. State and national public
relations efforts can be justified on this basis alone, but
there is a good deal more involved, too.

While it would be difficult to make a case for a direct

relationship between national publicity and the success of a particular college, there is no question that some of the most successful two-year institutions in the country are those that have received widespread publicity in their local communities, in the states, and nationally. Some of the big, city colleges come to mind instantly: St. Louis Community College District, Miami-Dade Community College, and Dallas County Community College District. But smaller, less urban-oriented institutions, too, have enjoyed national attention: Brevard in Florida, Johnson County Community College in Kansas, and Charles County College in Maryland. These institutions had two things going for them that made it possible for them to capture national attention: (1) they were of course doing an outstanding job of educating, in many cases innovating with facilities, teaching, and service to community, and (2) they had public relations operations that recognized opportunity when they saw it and got the word out to the right places. It is safe to say that the national visibility that they received was of assistance to them as they went to state legislatures and/or local voters for support. Local pride was operative.

There being no data to back up the assertion that national visibility results in greater local support, the question could reasonably ask whether the support might have come just as readily without a spread in *The New York Times* or a story in *The Wall Street Journal* or a mention on a TV special. What other reasons are there for spending some time and energy on public relations beyond the local community?

What attracts good faculty to a particular institution? Money? Locale? Mere happenstance? Dollars and locale may play a significant part in attracting faculty to a particular school, but reputation also is a major factor in selection of a place to teach. The institution that has a national reputation and is in the news beyond the local community may, as a result, have a better chance at getting the kind of faculty and staff it wants. Though in recent years post-secondary institutions have enjoyed a buyer's market in personnel, their job is made easier when they have a choice among good faculty rather than between the bad and the mediocre.

Today's students, skeptical of almost everything, judge their institution in the last analysis by its reputation or whether it is known at all. They, too, want to be proud of their college; they would rather attend a known than an unknown school. They can point with pride to an institution that has received some favorable national attention. Their vital support is more easily won.

The development function of an institution will be better served when that college or school has received some national visibility. Funding sources will be far more favorably inclined toward an institution that is known than toward one that is completely unknown. If a national publication, a prominent commentator, or a prominent businessman is on record as having accorded some recognition to the college's program, such information will help to open doors and to generate requested assistance. Successful fund-raising efforts of many institutions can be tied to their success in gaining favorable attention in the state and national media.

There is, perhaps, one other reason for the community-based institution to make a national public relations effort. If it is truly community based and service oriented, it will see an obligation to help improve the economic picture for the community and thus for itself. National attention for the college may help to lure new industry and business to a particular community. Often, national attention will simply come to the institution that is doing an outstanding job.

More often, however, some effort will have to be put forth to bring about the desired recognition.

The question is frequently raised, Should a community college which is part of a state system vie for attention with other parts of the system? Does it have any right to more attention than other colleges in the system? Will there be jealousies and bad feelings? There is only one answer. Colleges, even within a state system, are in some ways competitive. The college that shows greater initiative in its public relations effort, as well as in other parts of its program, will obviously gain more. One college's success nationally may, moreover, assist an entire system. There is no room for jealousy.

THE NATIONAL PUBLIC RELATIONS EFFORT

Alertness is perhaps the key to the public relations effort to obtain national attention for community colleges. The public relations staff must be alert to events, programs, and happenings on the campus that will attract favorable national attention, and the staff must be alert to national trends and developments that are currently making the news. Beyond that, the staff must be alert to the fact that national media are always interested in the unusual teacher or the student who is making good against great odds—the human interest element.

Community colleges certainly can compete with all kinds of institutions for national coverage. As service-oriented institutions, they are doing the kinds of things that make news and relate to national trends and developments. In recent years, community-based institutions have led the way in minority education, in veterans' programs, in environmental-control education, in health-related education, and in programs for the aging. Too often, awareness of what they have done in these areas has not gone beyond the local community. Public relations personnel have not taken advantage of the opportunities available to them to reach out for national attention.

Some may assume that to reach out requires tremendous effort beyond that of dealing with local media and that the extra effort would add too much to the already overburdened staff. True, additional time and energy must be budgeted for national public relations, but the task is not formidable. It is not some mysterious all-consuming activity. It simply calls for better planning and a more tailored and sophisticated operation. Perhaps a first step should be to look at the kind of media we are talking about.

If we are simply referring to national popular press and media, then we can narrow the universe to a half-dozen publications, four television networks, and five radio networks, two national wire services, a half-dozen feature syndicates, and a dozen or so individual columnists. But the huge spectrum of educational and professional journals, business-oriented publications, newsletters, and bulletins that represent important segments of the population should not be overlooked. They may be far more important, and far easier to crack, than the more popular media.

The Popular National Media

First of all, as a matter of course, press releases and/or publications dealing with college programs that relate to national trends and developments should be sent to the home offices of the national media. Though they will not frequently be used, many of the national editors and news directors maintain files that serve as background when they get around to doing a piece on a particular subject. It is useful, too, for the public relations chief to pay a visit at least once a year to headquarters offices of the national media, having in hand an idea for a story. Reporters and editors are usually open to such visits, although there should be much advance planning. Just as with the local press, it is important to get representatives of national media on campus. Many can and will accept invitations to address meetings or conferences. In the process, they may go away with a better impression of the institution, and perhaps a story idea.

Perhaps the best and least expensive route to the national popular media is through local and regional bureaus. *Newsweek, Time,* and *The New York Times,* maintain regional offices throughout the country. They often have stringers in larger cities. The public relations staff should know who they are, call on them occasionally, and again find ways to bring them to the campus of the institution. The regional representatives are paid to come up with interesting articles and to cover news in that region. They will be receptive.

National radio and TV, of course, are much more difficult to reach. Any viewer will readily note that very little time is devoted to education. However, educational stories often come out of the network affiliate in a particular community or region, so it is important to cultivate the news director or program director of such stations. There are many feature syndicates that look for the unusual or the offbeat story. Often the material they disseminate turns up in scores of newspapers and on radio news. A mere query and a brief story may result in coverage by such feature syndicates.

The wire services, United Press International and Associated Press, rely of course on local newspapers or their own bureaus for coverage. The services maintain bureaus in all state capitals and bigger cities, and they also have stringers, who may be on local newspapers. The public information officer should know these stringers and bureau people and make a special effort to bring stories to their attention.

National Columnists

In general, the national columnist has his own thing going and it is usually politically oriented. But they travel a lot and like to vary the political with the offbeat or the trend-setting situation. Many do give public speeches and are receptive to campus appearances. They may respond to a speaking invitation and pick up an idea for a column.

Business, Professional, and Educational Press

Community-based institutions look to the support of business and industry, of the professions, and of other elements of education, as they plan programs of training and education related to various fields and professions. Almost every profession, industry, and occupational area has some kind of publication, and there are many publications representing various aspects of education. Large and important special publics can be reached via this specialized national press. Most journals, newsletters, and bulletins representing the professions are wide open to articles that relate to their fields, either news items or full-scale articles on given subjects. The public relations office may simply serve as a conduit between a professional publication and a professional in the same field on the staff of the college, who will author the article.

Some practitioners may discount the importance of such media. Those who do will be missing an important opportunity to help build the college's reputation nationally in a particular field or fields, a reputation that may garner better understanding and thus result in more financial and moral support, and benefit graduates as well. If the hospitality industry, for example, recognizes a college for its work in that field, then students who complete programs in hospitality education will stand a better chance of entering the field. One way to build that recognition and reputation is to obtain attention in the media representing the field. There are directories that contain names of most professional and trade publications, but a query to the national office of a particular association will do just as well.

BRINGING THE NATIONAL SCENE TO THE COMMUNITY

Pasadena City College in California plays a key role in the annual Rose Bowl football game, particularly in the pregame activities and the Rose Bowl Parade. The parade, of course, as well as the football game, is seen by millions via the miracle of television. Pasadena City College traditionally provides the Rose Bowl Queen, who appears on a colorful float in the parade. College musical units also appear in the parade and at the game itself. The role of the college in bringing the Rose Bowl activities to Pasadena is lost in history. The point is, however, that the college has taken advantage of the circumstances set up by this colorful program to make certain that the national spotlight is focused on it for a few very telling minutes each year. Rose Bowl Parade national commentators sometimes interview officials of the college. When Pasadena musical units appear on camera, parade commentators provide background by describing the institution and its programs.

Obviously, Pasadena is the beneficiary of a very fortuitous situation. It simply happens to be at the right place at
the right time; national attention comes to the institution
because it's there. Very few schools and colleges will ever
be able to bask in the public relations benefits of a Rose
Bowl game and the attendant activities. But a community
college, a technical institute, or a private institution can
contrive to focus the national spotlight on the institution
and the community, and at the same time perform public
service. Prominent opinion leaders can be invited to schools
to give addresses. Often such speechmakers will make
pronouncements that bring attention to the institution; at
the same time, their performances benefit the community
by bringing it ideas and information. Community colleges
and other postsecondary institutions can stage events,
symposia, or forums that focus on national issues and thus
stand a chance of gaining national attention. Such programs
also contribute service and are justifiable on that basis.

It should not be assumed that the advantage is on the side
of an institution that is located in a large metropolitan area
or in a newsmaking community. In fact, that may not be
an advantage since institutions located in urban centers are
competing for attention with many other types of community organizations. The college that is located in Appa-
lachia, for example, can bring attention to the problems of
the poor in such an area through a symposium or a
demonstration that will stand out because there is lack of
competition for attention. Such issues as environmental
control, the plight of minorities, the energy problem, are
not confined to big cities; events related to them may, in
fact, have more impact in more isolated communities.
Obviously, staging of such events cannot be lightly under-
taken; they require careful, intensive planning. The positive
results hoped for must be weighed carefully against the

time, energy, and costs involved, but these are the elements that go into consideration of any public relations program from the lowliest press release to the most innovative activity.

As we have said, the national event or the activity calculated to produce national attention calls for careful planning. The first question is whether it will be worth the effort. Will the cost be prohibitive or will the activity actually provide financial support through the charging of admission fees or for the use of facilities? Is there any real hope that the program will result in national visibility, and if so, will such attention contribute to the positive image of the institution? Perhaps most important of all, does this activity contribute to the education and service dimensions of the school?

Should answers to these questions be affirmative, then the public relations staff, working with other departments that will actually have responsibility for the event, will work out plans to insure that maximum coverage results. Elements of the planning will include advance publicity locally and nationally, preparation of brochures and printed announcements, proper arrangements for guest speakers and/or participants, planning of press conferences during or after the event, duplication of speeches and/or reports to be made available to national media, and arrangements for press representatives who may come to the scene of the event. In some cases, the event may have public relations reverberations for some time to come. For example, a college or a cooperating agency may wish to publish a full-scale report some time after the event, perhaps long after the immediate attention has died down. That report may serve as a vehicle for followup meetings and it will serve as background material for in-depth reporting on the event.

There are obvious risks involved in using opportunities for serving as the setting for so-called national events. For example, many communities are not yet ready to accept organizations devoted to gay rights or legalization of pot. The discussion so far has been based on events that the college would officially generate, but there may be calls from the student body or faculty for use of the institution for different types of activities that may be far out. Sometimes the college may have little choice in the matter. Such situations call for a different kind of public relations activity, perhaps even an approach where the activity is actually played down, at least through official channels. If the institution proudly announces itself as community-based, then it may have no choice but to go all out on behalf of the event, meeting, or sympoisum involving an unpopular or questionable local group.

The point is that any college or school can be in the mainstream, regardless of its location or because of its setting. Alice Lloyd College in the hills of Kentucky has received a great deal of national attention because it is an institution that has been innovative and resourceful in serving poor whites; Malcolm X College, located in a Chicago ghetto, is well known nationally because it took new approaches to the education of blacks. Both institutions have received support as a result. Alice Lloyd and Malcolm X are extremes, but if two institutions that seemed to have everything against them could win important public relations battles, then why cannot other institutions with fewer negatives in their backgrounds win as well?

STEPPING OUT FOR NATIONAL
PUBLIC RELATIONS

The institution that is willing to permit its people to serve in national leadership roles—as speakers, as officers of organizations, as members of national committees and task forces—can gain national recognition. If its people are known as leaders, then the institution will be known as a leader. The public relations office, of course, is not in a position to make leaders of people or to elect them to national office, but it will take advantage of the public relations opportunities that emerge when a faculty member is elected to an office in the national organization of his or her discipline or vocation or profession. It will do everything it can to see that the honored person represents the institution well in his travels and speeches.

The public relations office may even have a more active role to play with regard to the chief administrative officer and other top officials of the institution. Its job is to look for opportunities to place the president and/or others on national programs and to advise officials on accepting or not accepting invitations to speak on national platforms or to serve on committees and task forces.

Flathead Valley Community College was not exactly a household name in places other than Kalispell, Montana, yet the institution became better known nationally and enjoyed increased support because its president accepted an invitation to serve as chairman of the National Council on Educational Professions Development, whose study and subsequent reports on faculty needs in community and junior colleges received widespread national press attention. The Flathead Valley president accepted the appointment because he was a concerned educator who saw in the invitation an opportunity to serve postsecondary education. He probably did not need or solicit public relations advice when the invitation came, but the public relations climate was such that he was able to take on the assignment. That is basically what this discourse is concerned with.

Many college presidents find the demand on their time and energy outside their daily administrative pursuits diffi-

cult. It is then that the public relations officer may be
called upon to help set up schedules and participate in
decisions about national assignments. He or she must take
into account the likelihood of public criticism that may
outweigh the advantages of the administrator taking on
speaking engagements and committee assignments in distant
places that will take him away from the campus for long
periods or very frequently. The public relations officer can
help the president to choose activities that will have the
greatest impact and perform the best service for the
president and the institution.

The national spotlight is valuable to the institution
which seeks to become viable, to lead, and to attract
attention that will result in greater support and interest,
but when the college loses sight of local goals while
pursuing national acclaim, then the advantage will be lost.
As in all things, moderation is important. Many community-based postsecondary institutions have been accused of
trying to become little Harvards. There is no future in that,
for it defeats the whole idea of what a community-based
institution is all about. Such an institution has something
to sell that Harvard or Princeton does not, and that's what
the public relations effort should concentrate on.

Going beyond the local scene will become more and
more important in the years ahead as more and more
opinion leaders, foundations, and the federal government
become aware of the attributes of two-year institutions of
postsecondary education, and as such institutions attempt
to share more fully in national resources that other institutions tend to take for granted. Public relations operations
will figure importantly in such programs and efforts.

Guidelines for Chapter 8 ⸻

I have tried herein to reason why the community, junior, or technical college can—and probably has an obligation to—beam its message to national audiences. Moreover, this chapter is intended to suggest that the scope of the public relations program rises to meet the aspirations of those responsible for it. This premise can be reduced to practical guidelines:

1. Community colleges are neglecting an important area in public relations if they overlook national visibility.
2. National attention will redound to the local scene, inspiring local pride that may result in greater local support, interest, and appreciation.
3. In the changing support picture for higher education, two-year postsecondary institutions need to become more competitive in terms of seeking national, state, and regional support and assistance.
4. Public relations planning should include concern with outlets for national media attention.
5. Public relations staff should be monitoring college programs that relate directly to national problems, trends, and issues for possible national coverage.

6. Colleges can take advantage of events and programs in their communities to which they can relate and which command national attention.

7. Community colleges can stage or become centers of national programs that will result in national visibility.

8. Community colleges will make certain that people in the institution, particularly top administrators, take advantage of opportunities for national leadership.

9. The total goal of national public relations efforts should be to insure that the institution shares fully in national resources that are available to all types of postsecondary educational institutions.

In Conclusion— A Challenge to the President _____ 9

"The decisions affecting the community, the image, the voice of the college, both externally and internally, must be worked out with the sensitive ear and hand of the public relations director. It must be a team approach. The director must be a member of the president's cabinet, sitting in on every top deliberation at every level of the college. Any lesser arrangement indicates that the institution doesn't really want a public relations director."

This comment, by Charles N. Pappas, president of Mott Community College, underscores one of my major contentions in this book. An effective public relations program depends for its being on the chief administrator's awareness and understanding of its importance. Without the wholehearted support and cooperation of the man or woman who heads the institution, there can be little hope for an organized, purposeful effort that will contribute to the well-being of the institution and the publics it serves. Moreover, understanding and backing means treating the office as a professional one on an equal basis with other administrative arms of the president's office. If the men and women directing public relations operations do not enjoy the same status in pay, titles, and perquisites that apply to persons heading other departments and offices of administration, they are not likely to have the respect and cooperation of others in top echelons of administration and of students and faculty. They will also find it difficult to carry on communications and relate to various colleges audiences if and when they are not accorded appropriate status.

Status and position, of course, must be earned. Just as deans of academic departments must meet certain educational requirements, so must public relations practitioners serve, either through experience and education, or a combination of both, apprenticeships that will prepare them for leadership in this important aspect of institutional management. There is a career ladder in this segment of administration just as there is in all others. There are exceptions, as suggested earlier, where a person without the usual formal communications skills required for the job may have an extraordinary grasp or sense of public relations, plus unusual connections, that will substitute for the usual training and experience.

PROFESSIONAL DEVELOPMENT

Along with proper status and recognition within the institution should come opportunity for professional development. Most other members of the administrative team are given opportunity and even encouraged to become involved in professional activities and organizations outside the college environs. The same kind of access to professional improvement should be provided for public relations staff, not only the chief executive of the office but others on the team as well. As a minimum, staff should be permitted and even urged to take part in state and regional meetings and workshops of organizations concerned with institutional advancement through such means as communications, community relations, and development. Such activities abound as increasing attention is focused on problems that require public relations input for their solution.

Members of the staff will also find it helpful to become
involved in national conventions and workshops conducted
by various professional organizations. Participation should
also include membership in groups concerned both with
professional development and with concerted efforts to
resolve common public relations problems. Certainly a small
share—which is all that is required—of the office planning
budget should be set aside for both membership and
participation in meetings. It is up to the vice-president or
director of public relations to determine priorities for
membership and for the chief administrator of the institution to cooperate in sanctioning such involvements.

Perhaps the best-known organization representing educational public relations practitioners is CASE, the Council
for the Advancement and Support of Education. CASE is a
product of the merger of two national organizations, the
American Alumni Council, and the American College Public
Relations Association. (That merger, incidentally, underscores
the fact that the many parts that go into advancement—public
information, alumni affairs, legislative relations, public relations, development, and publications—are logically organized into a whole for efficient and effective support of the
institutional message). Among other activities, the Council
provides workshops and a national assembly and engages in
a major communications program. A district organization
offers opportunities for members to consider regional problems and enjoy services that are geographically accessible.

Until recently, only a very small number of public
relations representatives of community colleges, technical
institutes, and other two-year units have taken part in
CASE activities, particularly at the national level. Some
have not taken part because of lack of recognition by the
chief administrator of their institutions of the importance
of this kind of professional development; this is an obstacle

which must be removed if these postsecondary institutions are to become effectively organized for the public relations job ahead. Other public relations representatives who may have requisite budgets for membership and travel object to what they feel is dominance by four-year colleges and universities of the offices and program. Those who do participate in the Council's activities do so because they feel that it is important to their professional development to become better acquainted with what other types of institutions are doing and to enjoy the many opportunities for interaction with representatives of those colleges and universities. The Council is vigorously recruiting persons from community, junior, and technical colleges. In recent years, its programs have reflected some concern with the special problems of two-year colleges, and both regional and national meetings provide opportunities for separate specialized meetings for representatives of two-year educational centers.

Two councils independent of CASE are operating specifically for persons employed in advancement at community, junior, and technical colleges. They are the National Council for Resource Development, and the National Council on Community Relations. Both organizations are affiliates of the American Association of Community and Junior Colleges and grew out of concern that the interests of the institutions in these important areas were not being well represented by existing professional organizations. Both are concerned with improving the professional skills of members, but they also tend to be action oriented.

The council for Resource Development, for example, assists the American Association of Community and Junior Colleges in bringing national attention to bear on important federal and state legislative issues. Some of its leadership have provided testimony on bills pending before Congress, and each year a national workshop in Washington provides opportunity for interaction with congressional and other government leaders. The Council has also been influential in organizing and cosponsoring with the Association a Washington internship experience in resource development for representatives of institutions from across country.

The Council on Community Relations, the newer of the two, sees as one of its major functions the counteracting or correcting of faulty images or perceptions of community-based education provided by two-year institutions of post-secondary education. In addition, the Council holds workshops and conducts a communications program to further professional development.

There is some overlap in the goals and purposes of the two councils. If one accepts the notion that all functions related to advancement should be integrated and organized under a central office, then one might well question the formation of two separate national councils to represent these interests. However, the councils have at least demonstrated the capacity to work closely together on larger advancement issues and concerns.

Finally, in exercising his or her responsibility to insure professionalism in the public relations office, the president will want to insist that public relations personnel seek additional training and education. Again, the situation is parallel with that of other administrators. Deans and heads of academic or occupational departments are expected periodically to refresh themselves, either through formal schooling or through independent projects. Public relations personnel require the same kinds of opportunities if they are to keep abreast of an ever-changing field and, above all, to be refreshed in their outlooks and perspectives. While some of this work can be done on the job, in general it will require the allocation of sabbatical time at periodic intervals. The allocation of such time at full salary will certainly pay for itself many times over, both in benefits to the institution and in the professionalization of the individual.

One obvious possibility for refreshment of view is course work in a major university where public relations programs are offered. Such educational work may not only add to the practitioner's ability to cope with his job but also will improve his or her status in the educational environment of the home college. Many universities also offer summer institutes and workshops in communications that may be of benefit.

Certainly one of the best ways to broaden horizons first hand is examination of practices in other institutions. A tour of selected colleges will provide the public relations officer with new insights into how others are conducting the work and dealing with issues. It will also give the official a chance to examine other programs and services of the colleges visited that may have application for the institution where she or he is employed.

The public relations officer may find it beneficial to be on the other side of the fence once in a while. Arrangements can sometimes be made with community groups, the media, or some national organizations for short internships through which the individual can gain new insight into some aspect of communications. Arrangements for such experiences must usually be worked out on an individual basis rather than through an organization or an educational institution.

An investigation of a particular problem or set of problems may provide still another channel for improving the perspective of the practitioner. Such a refresher activity can be accomplished through a survey or study or merely through a search of literature. The results may not only serve to assist the practitioner in his or her own job, but may also lend itself to publication whereby the information can be shared with personnel in other institutions.

Given the facts that management is part and parcel of the chief public relation officer's job and that the dimensions of the job involve all the elements of effective management, the officer should be urged if not required to improve skills in this area through participation in management seminars and workshops. All too often, lack of understanding of the latest management techniques and procedures causes public relations offices to operate somewhat more loosely and thus less effectively than other types of offices. Deadlines are not necessarily synonymous with objectives. Management is a vital ingredient in any plan of organization for public relations.

THE CONSULTING DIMENSION

Unlike more traditional four-year institutions, the newer postsecondary colleges and schools have as a rule acknowledged the need to expose themselves to outside review and examination. In virtually every area of activity they have called upon consultants and advisors for assistance. Most, for example, use advisory committees to help plan curriculums. They bring in experts in counseling, faculty development, and general planning for assistance in insuring that techniques and methods match commitment. It is another challenge for the college president to recognize that neither he nor his staff may have all the answers or expertise needed for the job.

College relations, like the other areas of administration and operations, bears constant review and revision. One of the least expensive ways to receive guidance is to obtain outside counsel. Sometimes the appraisal may be disturbing, sometimes disappointing, but it usually either confirms questions that may be in the chief executive's mind or helps buttress planning for effective public relations. The public relations office need not normally view such counsel as a threat or a problem, because, in more cases than not, the reviewers or consultants will blame weak budgets or poor planning by the board and the executive rather than the public relations office itself. If the public relations staff is over concerned, it is probably because they have doubts about the effectiveness of their work.

Unlike instructional techniques or counseling performance consultants, public relations consultants must be urged to conduct their interviews largely with people not performing the formal functions of public relations; a quick review of the techniques used by the public relations office and the products resulting should do. Having the consultants talk to those affected by public relations is a better use of time and money. They should be urged to talk with representatives of local media, with trustees, faculty, students, business people, and tradesmen. The opinions and perceptions of these audiences will give a far more accurate picture of the effectiveness of the public relations program than could be gained from looking at newsletters, memoranda, or press releases. If these and other devices and techniques are not stimulating appropriate images among the college's audiences, then something obviously is awry. It is up to the president, of course, to set the stage and steer the right course for the consultant team. While the experts may have a plan of action that they tend to follow, it may not be appropriate for the particular institution. Consultant time is costly; it should not be wasted.

SAMPLING PUBLIC OPINION

As we said in an earlier chapter, there is no easy way to evaluate the effectiveness of the public relations job being done. In years past, a fat, press-clipping book was a standard measurement, but the number of press releases used by the media does not give a single clue as to how the message is received and what action is generated. Evaluation is easier for fund-raisers. Whether or not they achieve the goals they set is some indication of impact and success. Public opinion polling can help in evaluating the rest of the public relations program.

Community-based institutions of postsecondary education, as we have seen, must have strong connections with various publics in their services areas and these connections should provide ready tools for ascertaining how people perceive the institution, its programs, and its objectives. Leadership of the various publics can easily be persuaded to organize citizens to take samples by telephone or written communication. Considerable use can also be made of the immediate college family. Faculty with expertise in survey methods should be called upon for input into the planning and conducting of public opinion sampling. Such sampling efforts also pose opportunities for actual class assignments in such courses as psychology, sociology, and communications, or a combination thereof. Organized student groups can also be invited to participate in this kind of activity. Public opinion polling need not be complicated and cumbersome. Questions should be brief and few. They should be pointed.

Whether a poll is designed to gather general information on how its constituents perceive the college or whether it is aimed at determining attitudes toward a particular program or service, the results should prove extremely useful to the administration—including the public relations staff—in carrying out institutional purposes. In some cases objectives might well be changed as a result of negative impressions or positive proposals that come from the public. This, too, is a challenge for the president, for it is far easier for him to maintain the status quo than to be open to change in response to public criticism or questions that may even reflect on the performance of executives, the board, or other members of the college family. The results of public opinion polls should be treated as aids to the institution, not as targets.

IN THE FINAL ANALYSIS

Public relations is a challenge for the chief administrator of the community-based postsecondary institution of education, whether it be a community college, a technical institute, a private junior college, a branch campus or a university, or a two-year proprietary institution. Organizing and carrying out an effective public relations program is also a great opportunity to contribute to the improvement of the quality of life in the towns, urban centers, rural communities and suburban complexes which are increasingly served by two-year colleges, schools, and institutes.

To advance the institution, and in the end to improve the quality of life, requires the understanding that begets cooperation and support. In a society that grows more complex from year to year, communication is vital. No institution, agency, government, or organization can expect to realize its promise or its objectives if it does not clearly and aggressively make known what it stands for, what it has to offer, and where it is going. The president of the community-based postsecondary institution is faced with increasingly heavy pressures on his time and energy. An effective public relations program will go far toward relieving many of those awesome pressures.

Index _____